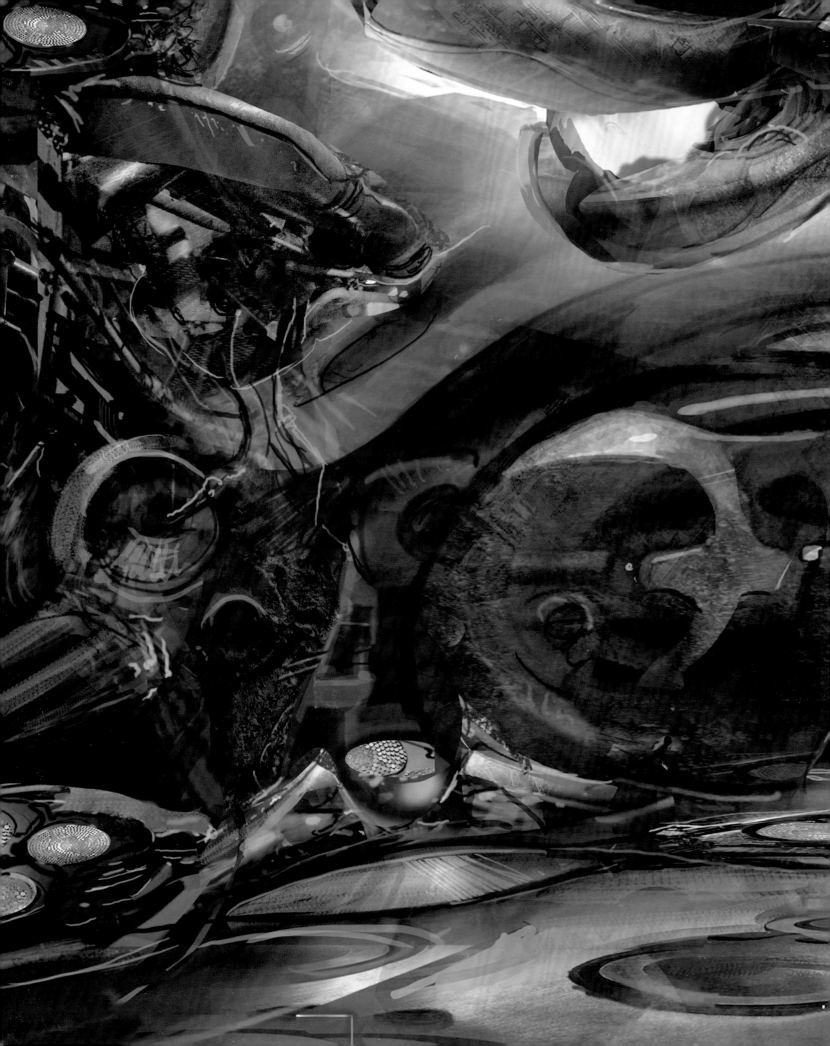

MAN OF STEEL

INSIDE THE LEGENDARY WORLD OF **SUPERMAN**

BY DANIEL WALLACE
PHOTOGRAPHY BY CLAY ENOS
STORY BY DAVID S. GOYER & CHRISTOPHER NOLAN
SCREENPLAY BY DAVID S. GOYER
BASED UPON SUPERMAN CHARACTERS CREATED BY
JERRY SIEGEL & JOE SHUSTER AND PUBLISHED BY DC ENTERTAINMENT
BY SPECIAL ARRANGEMENT WITH THE JERRY SIEGEL FAMILY

INSIGHT ◉ EDITIONS

San Rafael, California

CONTENTS

FOREWORD

CHRISTOPHER NOLAN

SUPERMAN. SUPER MAN. A name, the very name, of heroism itself. Much imitated, never bettered, for the exact reason of the concept's absolutism—the most powerful heroic figure ever created. A modern myth, a modern Greek God, but one with no equals, no peers. A universe of Super Heroes grew up around him, but Superman lets these others believe themselves to be in his league only because he knows that no one quite forgets that he was created as a singular heroic figure—the absolute peak of perfection by which any other hero must be compared, and found wanting. Only Batman was allowed to gain a similar foothold in the popular imagination, because Batman was not a competing God, merely the best hero that mankind could throw in the Man of Steel's wake. Surely, then, Superman is the most obvious of all heroic figures to put on the big screen?

Richard Donner cracked it for my generation with his seminal blockbuster *Superman: The Movie*, the title of which said everything about the promise of a match between icon and popular medium. But how to present Superman to a new generation of moviegoers? When David Goyer and I first traveled to the New York offices of DC Comics to tell them of our plans to re-envisage the Dark Knight, our pitch was warmly received by then-president Paul Levitz. He explained that Batman had thrived under continuing reinterpretation, however radical, then added:

"Superman, of course, less so." His words came back many times as I tried to help David realize his dream of recrafting the Superman legend for today's audiences.

Science Fiction were the words at the core of the pitch. Ground the tale by dealing head-on with the implications of an alien walking among us. This exciting idea needed a visual magician—a filmmaker who could throw the audience into a fully realized alien culture they could embrace within seconds. Zack Snyder had shown an extraordinary grasp of the technical complexities and heightened storytelling demanded by this genre in both *300* and *Watchmen*. We were thrilled when he agreed to take this on. Particularly thrilled because we could see how reluctant he was. He understood the responsibility and wanted to run away—but his love for the character won out.

I believe that what Zack has done in *Man of Steel* will define Superman for our time, but there is little point in describing Zack's infectious enthusiasm in words when the incredible images in these pages get it across so magnificently. I've seen a lot of concept art in my time, but I've rarely seen such focused visual power. And I've rarely seen the promise of such imagery actually delivered onto the screen. But that's what Zack does.

INTRODUCTION

ZACK SNYDER

THE SINGLE POINT AT WHICH everything we know and everything we question exist in one place; the ultimate crossroads in the journey of discovering the true meaning of "self"; the collision point of science and religion, tangible and ethereal, physical and philosophical; the place where a question that may never truly have an answer can be embodied in a singular character—in many ways, that is the *why* of Superman.

In my mind, the coolest part about the character of Kal-El/Clark Kent is that his alien origins, combined with his Smallville upbringing, simultaneously make him entirely relatable and completely mysterious. This duality allows us to look at ourselves through the prism of Clark, embracing that which we understand and forcing us to acknowledge and accept that which we don't yet comprehend. Although the challenges facing Clark may be much more interplanetary than our own, the reality is that those sometimes overwhelming difficulties we each struggle to reconcile as we grow—especially throughout our youth—often feel just as immense as being from another planet.

Seventy-five years ago, Kandor and Kansas collided, giving birth to one of the most storied characters of all time—Superman—a single character who calls into question everything we believe. Whether it is the belief that we humans are the apex of an evolutionary process, the pinnacle of God's creation, or anything else along the complex spectrum where science and theisms grapple for space, Superman challenges all of those ideas to their core. He forces us to look at ourselves as individuals, and mankind as a whole, through the filter of a being who looks very much like us but has the physical strength and abilities of a god. Yet, despite his corporeal strengths he is not omniscient, and therefore must venture out into the world on his own journey of self-discovery. No more able to see the future than any of us, and in many ways much less aware of his past than most, he is in essence a lost god. A deity forced to walk the Earth alone, seeking his own personal truth while inadvertently calling into question the very truths the rest of mankind cling to so tightly.

That was the challenge that I found most interesting when I decided to take on *Man of Steel*. I was enthralled by the amazing opportunity to place this helplessly divine figure firmly in our imperfect world. It was a chance to tell the complicated story of a struggling savior, a reluctant messiah, in a modern way. An opportunity to carefully deconstruct the classic godlike character, who we have often perceived as aspirational but also distant and divine at times. Allowing the audience to walk alongside Clark during his formative years—matching stride with him as a child, a teen, and ultimately a young man—creates a bond that perseveres even as that man becomes mythological in stature. That initial kinship is what lets us as humans experience the transformative process of the character from an incredibly close proximity, ultimately helping us to both understand and relate to the evolution of Clark Kent into Superman.

Making *Man of Steel* has been an amazing journey. As a filmmaker, I consider it an honor to have the opportunity to lovingly deconstruct and reassemble such a beloved character and rich imaginative world. I'm thrilled to have been able to immerse myself in seventy-five years of legend and lore, and I am now excited to share with you my own journey in building upon the already mythological world of

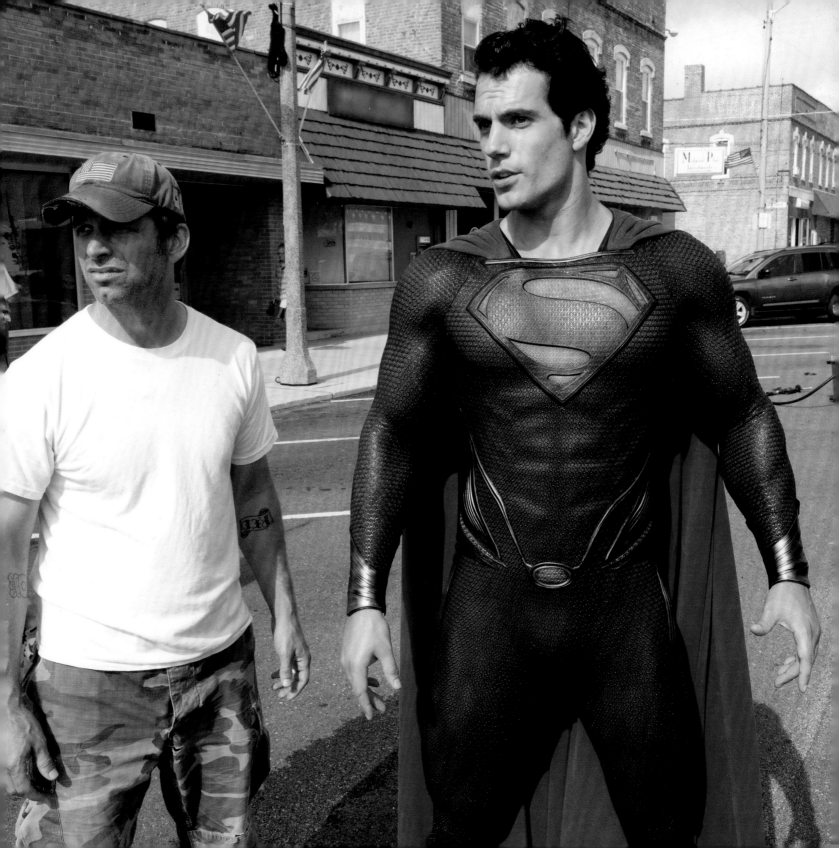

SUPERMAN™ WAS THE VERY FIRST SUPER HERO, and he's still the most famous. When *Action Comics* #1 hit newsstands in 1938, none of its Depression-era buyers could have guessed that the figure on the cover—the colorful one lifting a sedan above his head—represented the birth of an American genre.

Everything about Superman, including his red cape, his Clark Kent alter ego, and his ties to Lois Lane and the *Daily Planet*, is pop-cultural currency. Everyone can repeat the catchphrases: *Up, up, and away! Faster than a speeding bullet!*

Those elements are all drivers of the Superman phenomenon, and have helped make the character a sort of cultural shorthand who can stand in for the concepts of strength, sacrifice, and secret identities. But the creators of *Man of Steel* wanted to take Superman's familiar exterior and go much deeper. They didn't want to simply depict an icon, but to explore the complex story behind the man.

"Superman, he's the king of all Super Heroes," says director Zack Snyder. "He exists in a weird way outside of geek culture, and outside of comic book culture. He always was that sort of golden god upon a hill."

Christopher Nolan co-wrote and directed *The Dark Knight Trilogy*, which restored Batman as a cinematic icon. Nolan developed the story for *Man of Steel* with writer David Goyer, and approached the task by carefully considering the roles that heroes are meant to fill. "One of the big differences between Superman and Batman is that, while they're both very theatrical, Batman is a darker character," he says. "You can hide some of that theatricality in the shadows, literally as well as metaphorically, and there are darker places to go to help offset that fact.

"But Superman is a much tougher character to crack. He's out there in the blazing sunshine, and he has to be so direct. I grew up in the late '70s when Richard Donner made the terrific *Superman: The Movie,* where he was put up on the screen as the biggest character in the world. It made a massive impression on me, and presented the character as extremely aspirational."

Batman's darkness and Superman's decency are prime archetypes within the Super Hero genre. When Snyder's passion for costumed heroes tempted him to explore them further to deconstruct their appeal, he explored similar themes in 2009's *Watchmen*, his adaptation of the influential graphic novel that came with its own heroic archetypes. In this cinematic setting, both the omnipotent Dr. Manhattan and the handsome Ozymandias represented character elements that had sprung from Superman's template.

"My favorite character in *Watchmen* was Dr. Manhattan," says Snyder. "To me, he's like Superman evolved. One of my favorite lines [in the film] is 'Superman's real, and he's American.' We have the bomb, is what they're saying. And we think of these ultimate weapons as faceless and having no heart."

But these Superman-influenced characters can never be the same as the genuine article, and the Man of Steel was always more than just a guided missile. The analogy of Superman as an atomic bomb was always an incomplete one, since it ignored the character's compassion. And while Snyder knew his fan credentials on Superman were solid, he wasn't going to touch the character unless he had something to say. "When your English teacher says you've got to know the rules before you can break them, in a weird way that's what *Watchmen* was in reverse," he says. "It made me really have to study the rules of the Super Hero genre. And for me, it's about taking Super Hero mythology seriously. The way I feel about Superman is that I accept him as American mythology, in the same way that mythology was created by the ancient Greeks as a response to power struggles or a way of explaining and dealing with a fear.

PAGES 14–15: Superman looks down at the city he must save in this piece captured from the POV of a street-level onlooker.

LEFT: The façade of the Metropolis courthouse crumbles and Superman can only watch, in this piece depicting the threat to "truth and justice."

"I think Superman is born from those same responses, whether they are the Cold War, World War II, or Jewish immigrants trying to find their way in America. As long as there's an atmosphere of mutual respect between an audience and a character, you can be serious and you can express other things."

That didn't mean taking the character to extremes of gritty violence or winking irony. Dealing with Superman meant playing it straight. "Superman, he has rules," says Snyder. "And those rules are there for a reason."

It's that attention to the canon that has landed Superman atop the comic book pantheon of gifted gods. And, because of his alpha status, Superman has sometimes been portrayed as impossibly virtuous. Yet the character comes from two worlds and bears two names. He is simultaneously Kal-El, the son of Jor-El and Lara, the last child of Krypton, and Clark Kent, a midwestern farm boy raised by Jonathan and Martha Kent in Smallville, Kansas.

Producer Charles Roven, whose notable career includes all three films in *The Dark Knight Trilogy*, came to *Man of Steel* with

the understanding that the title character would only work on screen by taking a realistic approach that united the disciplines of world-building, filming, and casting. "The whole approach to Superman was to make him feel that he truly could exist somewhere on our planet today," he says.

"Clark has always had sort of a very clean-cut, almost naïve persona," says co-producer Wes Coller. "I think part of what the were able to successfully do in scripting the film, and then in Zack's casting and shooting, is create a character that is rugge and in a lot of ways a 'guy's guy.' Just your typical guy that's relatable and pretty down to earth."

OPPOSITE: A costuming mockup depicts Russell Crowe as Jor-El, wearing his Kryptonian battle armor and carrying a heavy weapon. The breastplate bears the crest of the House of El.

ABOVE: Teardrop-shaped petals form an interlocking footpath through the heart of the buried scout ship.

ABOVE: Concealed beneath the floorboards of the Kent family barn is the spacecraft that brought Kal-El to Earth, further shrouded beneath a dusty tarp in this concept art painting.

OPPOSITE: Superman perches atop a train's engine, which now protrudes from the side of a skyscraper. It is a sign of the devastation that can happen if tremendous power isn't kept in check.

Zack Snyder agrees in part, adding, "I think in the early versions of Superman he was morally clear. But as society has become more open and we've been able to talk about the skeletons in our closets, Superman was strangely not involved in that conversation. We all moved on to darker Super Heroes who were more emotionally complex. But he's an orphan, he's got issues, he's complicated, and it's hard being Superman."

When everything else has been stripped away from the character, what's left is empathy. Among all of pop culture's Super Heroes, it is Superman who has the biggest heart.

"Superman is sensitive to a fault when it comes to humanity and mankind," says Snyder. "He is truly the adopted son. His involvement with humanity even trumps his Kryptonian origins. Jor-El says the people of Earth are different and their capacity to love is greater. Earthlings are weaker, but in a way they have the capacity to be greater than the Kryptonians as people."

Because Superman is the product of both Krypton and Earth, he has the potential to be the greatest of all.

MAKING IT HAPPEN

With *The Dark Knight Trilogy*, Christopher Nolan had demonstrated that it was possible to dynamically reinterpret a Super Hero for modern moviegoers. After reinvigorating the Batman legend, Nolan and his collaborator David Goyer put their talents into developing a film treatment that dealt with perhaps the most famous hero of them all.

Goyer first shared his concept for *Man of Steel* while he and Nolan worked on the story for *The Dark Knight Rises*. "He was describing a science-fiction based approach to update the Superman story for the next generation," says Nolan. "And I thought it was a terrific start. I had been somewhat skeptical as to how you could take a character as fanciful as Superman and make him work for a contemporary audience. And I got involved because I really wanted to see that version of *Man of Steel* get made."

Nolan's wife, producer Emma Thomas, recalls pitching the idea to the studio with the full understanding that they would need to pass *Man of Steel* into the hands of a different filmmaker. "We were at the point where we were going to start making *The Dark Knight Rises*," she says. "It was time for us to step back and let someone else really make it their own. We wanted to find a filmmaker who could capture that Americana and incredible positivity of Superman, what he is and what he means to the world."

The handoff occurred at thirty-five thousand feet, even if neither party knew it yet. Aboard an airliner bound for Las Vegas, Christopher Nolan and Emma Thomas shared the cabin with fellow husband-and-wife team Zack and Deborah ("Debbie") Snyder. Business had brought them together, as both readied presentations for upcoming films at 2010's ShoWest Convention. But it was Superman who would make the partnership blossom.

"They were there with *Inception*, and we were there with our animated film *Legend of the Guardians*," remembers Debbie Snyder. "It was the first time we had met them, and we said we'd have a meal when things settled down. And then we got a call from them. They said, 'Would you like to have lunch? And by the way, would you mind talking about Superman?'"

At that point in development, Christopher Nolan and David Goyer had generated an early screenplay. "I remember saying to Zack, 'This is going to be a mistake,'" admits Debbie Snyder. "'How do you do this?' I just thought he was a really hard character to get at."

But the Snyders took the Nolans up on their offer, and over lunch they listened to the details of their vision. "Sitting with Zack as we pitched him on what we thought this film could be, I was very keen to see if this was a film he wanted to get involved with," remembers Nolan. "Because as a director myself, I know what a huge challenge taking on a character like Superman represents. It's something you have to get right. From our experiences on the Batman films, these are characters that the fans become so protective of. And so I was certainly worried that he might not want to take on this huge challenge."

Emma Thomas saw signs of promise. "We talked it through with Zack and Debbie and why we thought Zack should be the director," she says. "I think he really did feel a connection with the story. We felt really good about them and were thrilled at the chance to put it into their hands so they could make it their own."

Hollywood veterans know that good vibes can evaporate quickly once the actual product is put under scrutiny. "I remember saying to Zack, 'I hope the script is as good as what Chris just pitched us,'" she says. "'Because if it is, he just figured out a way to make Superman fit for a modern audience.'"

Given the level of secrecy surrounding the project, the *Man of Steel* screenplay made its way to the Snyders' doorstep at 7 a.m., with a messenger waiting in their driveway while they finished reading it. "They really figured out how to get at this character in a different way, in a way that you could care about him and in a way that he could be cool," says Debbie Snyder. "And then we said, 'Oh no—now we have to deal with the suit.'"

Producer Charles Roven joined the team during the start-up stage, bringing his expertise to the table to help figure out solutions to the practical problems they would soon face. "The first draft of the script was written, but I came onto the film very shortly after Zack

OPPOSITE: Henry Cavill films a key sequence in *Man of Steel*.

LEFT: When super-strength meets invulnerability, even the solid steel of a bank vault will crumple.

and Debbie," he says. "From that point on, particularly with Chris and Emma focused primarily on *The Dark Knight Rises*, the day-to-day collaboration for mounting the film was handled by the three of us."

Man of Steel began early preproduction, or "soft prep," in October 2010 with the hiring of key personnel in production and costume design By January the crew had moved into "hard prep," expanding department staffing and scrambling to run through a rapidly approaching gauntlet o deadlines for the planned start of shooting in August 2011.

The decision was made; the principals were committed. Now the team prepared to turn a story into a vision and bring Superman back to cinemas. "Our films have always been polarizing, and they've always been risky choices," says Debbie Snyder. "And that's exciting. For me I would rather make a film that people talked and argued about than a film that no one cared about."

MAKING IT REAL

Zack Snyder's body of work is famous for strikingly stylized visuals, from *300* to *Watchmen* to *Sucker Punch*. But *Man of Steel* offered a different challenge. Though Snyder was no stranger to comic book source material, he aimed to present the ultimate comic book character in a manner that erased the distance between the viewer and the viewing experience. From handheld cameras to meticulous world-building, the *Man of Steel* crew operated under the mantra of *making it real*.

"Our approach was not necessarily to do a *dark* Superman, just to do a more realistic Superman," explains writer David Goyer. "Not a comic book version, but a Superman that exists in a real world. We're trying to make the movie feel very visceral. Superman already is a character that exists outside the bounds of reality, but we're trying as hard as possible to make the movie feel grounded."

Christopher Nolan didn't want to dictate a particular approach for how Zack Snyder might bring the story to life. "But the thing that I did keep emphasizing is that we wanted the character to be relatable and grounded," he says. "I had no idea how Zack was going to take that on, but I think he is one of the great visual directors of this generation."

Debbie Snyder was all too aware of the fact that Super Hero films have become a genre unto themselves, often possessing similar aesthetics and shared story beats. "Sometimes they feel very period," she says, "or sometimes they're very stylized. We wanted to do the opposite of that. We wanted it to feel real, we wanted the drama to feel real. And that was all in an effort to make [Superman] as relatable as possible."

THESE PAGES: Superman prepares for one of the greatest fights of his life as he faces Zod's insurgents on the streets of Smallville.

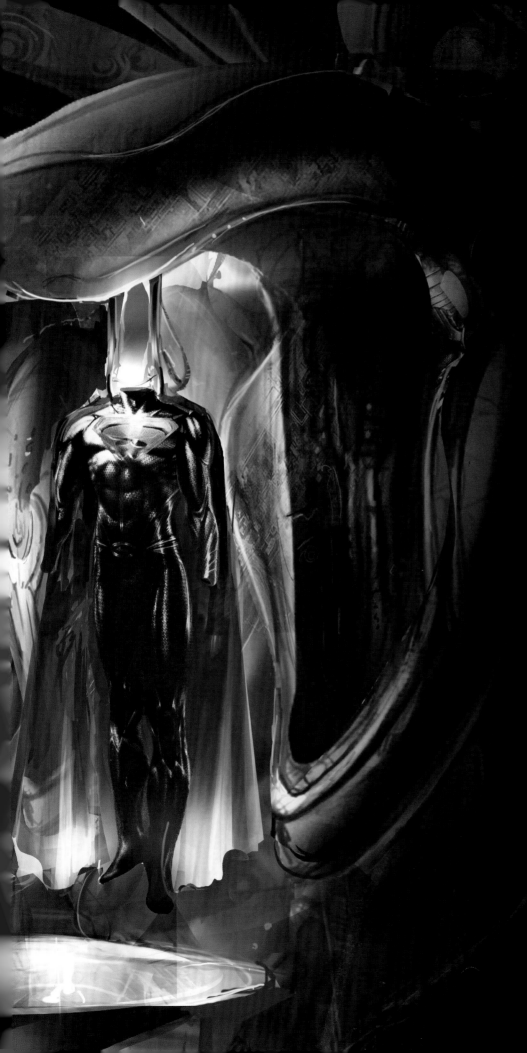

THE SUIT

If you're working with Superman, you've got to start with the suit. But how can you completely reinvent one of the classics of costume design? For Zack Snyder, it was an easy answer: You don't.

Snyder saw no need to toss out the fundamentals, even as designers brought him ideas that veered into blue jeans and casual street clothes. In Snyder's mind's eye, the key elements remained: primary colors of red, yellow, and blue; a trim silhouette defined by a barrel chest and a hanging cape; high boots; and a triangular chest emblem inscribed with the familiar letter *S*.

One thing didn't survive, however. As Snyder notes, a big reason why the "underwear on the outside" look no longer seems fresh is the fact that it dates from the nineteenth century. "Strong men [would] have a flesh-colored leotard on," he explains. "Then they'd put the underwear over it, to make it look like all [they] had on was underwear. That's basically where Superman comes from; the reason why his underwear is on the outside of his pants is because it's a leftover from Victorian-era strong men. I couldn't make it consistent with the world we were creating."

With that minor tweak in place, costuming could begin in earnest. "We interviewed a number of costume designers and had boiled it down to two," Charles Roven explains. "Zack had worked with Michael Wilkinson on *Sucker Punch* and *Watchmen*, but Michael wasn't immediately available. James Acheson was and he was fantastic, and came up with a significant portion of the designs for *Man of Steel*, preliminary designs for the Kryptonian armor, and the whole concept of the [chest] glyph being both a family symbol and a Kryptonian symbol. And when for personal reasons he suddenly had to leave the show, fortunately Michael Wilkinson had become available."

For Snyder, interpreting the *S* symbol was like paging through an illuminated manuscript, an act deserving both reverence and care. Superman's insignia has gone through many variations over the decades, but Snyder found himself drawn to the version Superman wore during World War II, which featured graceful lines resembling art nouveau.

"I like to draw on that [era] as much as I can, because I feel he was born again after World War II," explains Snyder. "He came to represent the American fighting machine and the way America exported its morality to the world. I was drawn to that, and I wanted to get back to a slightly more elegant and more graphically sophisticated *S*."

THESE PAGES: On the inside, the Kryptonian scout ship resembles the innards of a living creature. Pods contain Kryptonian skinsuits, ready for use by the ship's crew.

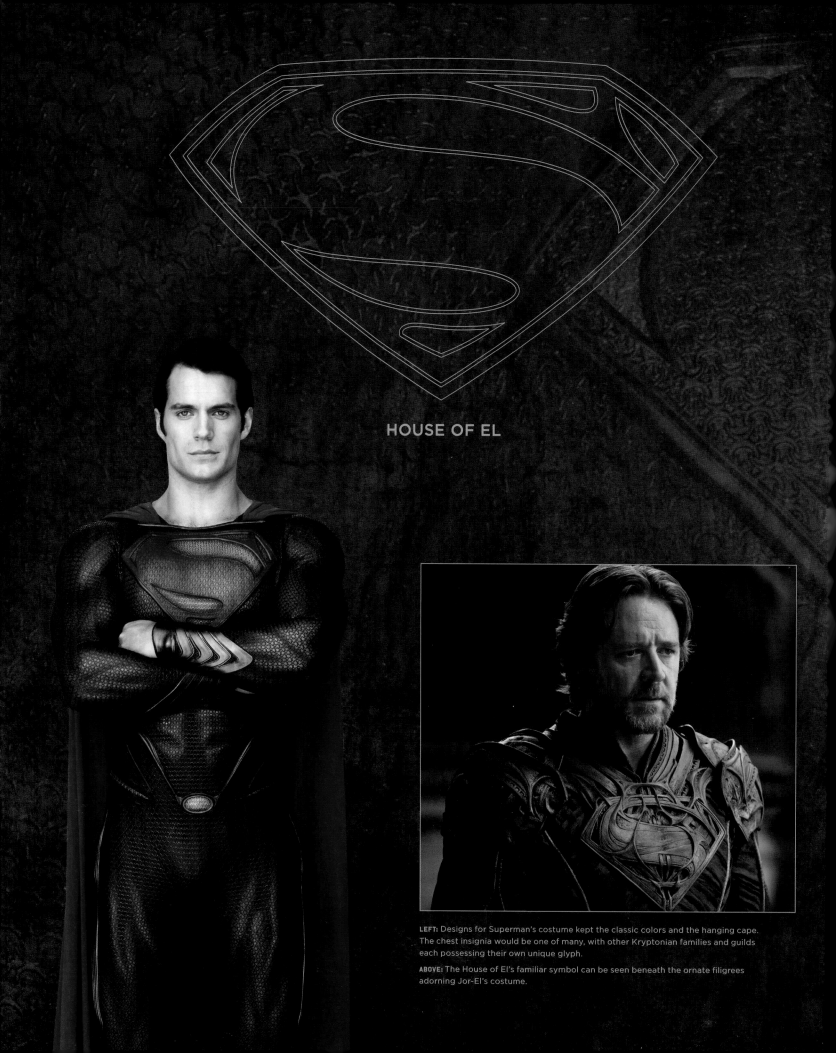

HOUSE OF EL

LEFT: Designs for Superman's costume kept the classic colors and the hanging cape. The chest insignia would be one of many, with other Kryptonian families and guilds each possessing their own unique glyph.

ABOVE: The House of El's familiar symbol can be seen beneath the ornate filigrees adorning Jor-El's costume.

Lor-Em
THINKER GUILD

Council #2
LABORER GUILD

Council #1
WARRIOR GUILD

Ro-Zar
MEDIATOR GUILD

Ceremonial / Sapphire Guards
CITY OF KANDOR GLYPH

Aristocrat #1

Aristocrat #2

Aristocrat #3

Aristocrat #6

Aristocrat #4

Nam-Ek

Council #3
ARTISAN GUILD

When Michael Wilkinson picked up the baton from Acheson, he turned his artwork into a tangible supersuit with sheen and texture. "It's like what a chainmail suit is to the knights of medieval times," Wilkinson says. "If you look closely, it has the chainmail motif that covers the whole body. We looked a lot at medieval heraldry and the sort of iconic symbols of dynasties and guilds."

Other influences present in the finished suit include elements from Celtic and Japanese design. "We have a beautiful streamlined detail, [going] through the sides of his rib cage and the details on his cuffs," Wilkinson points out.

The costuming department also generated a digital body scan and produced a full-body cast, used for precise fitting to the actor's exact proportions. They also made a 3-D computer model of the suit to mirror various components and ensure perfect symmetry. "We could go in there and bevel every last 1/32 of an inch," he says. "We knew that the camera would see every last square inch of the Superman suit."

The detailing of the suit material might look like the interlocking links of a chainmail tunic, but the costume's backstory revealed its role as a sci-fi skinsuit that could protect its wearer from the vacuum of space. "It's a really high-tech kind of fabric, which I think is a nice departure from the spandex," says Debbie Snyder. The color choices also underscored the theme of fathers and sons, with Jor-El wearing a similar ensemble. "The House of El, their color is blue, so Jor-El has this suit in blue."

These touches helped put the suit into the larger societal context of Krypton, and Zack Snyder felt that it served as a symbol of the lost heritage that a curious Kal-El sought out. "It's a cultural experience, finding his Superman identity," he says. "The costume is a cultural link; almost by default, it becomes his Super Hero costume. [But] Jor-El did not *design* him to be a Super Hero. How could he know that Earth needed a hero like that?"

Michael Wilkinson also faced the challenge of costuming Clark Kent. Both characters, of course, have identical body proportions, but Wilkinson aspired to make them distinct visual experiences. "We really wanted to have that sense of hiding," he says, in discussing Clark's look as he ventures into the frozen north. "He wears many layers. You don't really see who he is. He has his hat down low. He has his beard. He kind of really blends in with the rest of the world."

Of course, Clark is far from an ordinary guy. When he sheds his concealing layers, viewers get glimpses of the hero beneath. "He really has an interesting kind of visual arc throughout the film," says Wilkinson. "[The suit has] a whole different silhouette and it really affects how he walks and moves."

SUPERMAN VÉRITÉ

Movies with fantastical elements can sometimes be captured through stylized camerawork and elaborate shots. It's something Zack Snyder advanced through his own cinematic style, by making films like *300* and *Sucker Punch* look both otherworldly and distinctive. But with *Man of Steel*, Snyder had something different in mind.

Snyder's decision to pursue a vérité style on *Man of Steel* broke new ground for big-budget Super Hero blockbusters. This approach would free the camera from the locked-down vantage points of tripods and wheeled dollys, instead going with a naturalistic handheld style to shake up the film's visual language. Under director of photography Amir Mokri and camera operator John Clothier, *Man of Steel* aimed to suggest the "you are there" point of view of modern photojournalism. The decision to shoot on film, not digitally, helped give the movie its classic moving-image aesthetics. "I've only ever shot on film," says Snyder. "I feel that film is richer and warmer and I'm sure a lot of people would debate that, and that's fine. But in this case, my vision was the one that counted. I'm glad we shot it on film, because I feel it really brings out that cinematic quality."

"How would it feel to the audience to be Superman?" asks Zack Snyder. "It's an approach that really has not existed up till now; because Superman is such a godlike figure it would be like saying, 'What would it feel like to be Zeus?' To render that emotionally, the setting needs to jive with that. That subtext allows you to go, 'That's a setting I'm familiar with,' and so you become more empathetic with the character and the choices he has to make."

But a handheld camera didn't mean going to the herky-jerky extremes associated with the "found footage" genre. "Zack did it in a very organic way that sometimes used a longer lens," says Debbie Snyder, "or sometimes the camera would just slightly move, just so it felt not so pristine and composed. That gave the sense that you were there."

This hybrid style pleased Charles Roven, who thinks *Man of Steel* benefited from the best of all possible styles: "We still had our dolly shots and our crane shots and our amazing camera-mount shots. But [for] the far majority . . . there's actually a guy who's handholding the camera at the end of all that. It's not stuck on a mount."

During filming, this meant that John Clothier had to put in a sometimes athletic performance. Cast members described him as a "human gyroscope" as he circled them with his camera and bravely walked backward down staircases. Yet he remained as unobtrusive as possible, earning praise for what actress Amy Adams (Lois Lane) calls his "very monk-like, very Zen" approach.

Roven emphasizes that the vérité style didn't stop at the camera's lens. "It was the inspiration of Zack from the moment he read the script," he says. "Because the character was written that way, when we were casting for the actors Zack would take great pains to make sure that they understood that that was the direction he was taking."

Henry Cavill soon joined the team as *Man of Steel*'s Superman, and he quickly got accustomed to the nontraditional approach. "What are people going to experience with the combination of Amir, Zack, and John?" Cavill asks. "I think they're going to feel like they're there. When I watch the footage, I feel like I'm a voyeur on this stuff that I just did."

After developing the story and welcoming Zack Snyder on board, Christopher Nolan left *Man of Steel* in the director's capable hands as he began shooting *The Dark Knight Rises*. He kept in touch as the film steamed ahead. "Zack would call me up from time to time with a question about an interpretation of a scene to get my mind on that," he says. The first time he saw the visual approach that Snyder had taken, he was impressed by its naturalism. "I thought it was incredibly apt," he says. "He took on the reality of the story, in the texture of the world reflected in the photography and the design. And as a viewer it makes me relate to the character of Clark and Superman in a way that I hadn't felt before."

Emma Thomas took a similar *Dark Knight Rises* detour, returning just in time to see how concepts had been fleshed out. "It was an incredible experience because we'd gone off on our own journey," she says. "And when we came back much of it was done, and there was Henry Cavill in the Superman costume. It was like all my dreams came to life."

OPPOSITE: Zack Snyder captures Cooper Timberline for the camera, his makeshift cape hinting at a greater destiny for Clark Kent.

HENRY CAVILL ⚡ SUPERMAN

Actor Henry Cavill is British through and through, and yet, Superman, of course, is as American as apple pie. Superman, however, is also a strange visitor from another planet, and Cavill possessed a trustworthiness and decency that felt more integral to the core of the character than his birthplace or his chiseled physical perfection.

"Henry has traveled the world, and our Superman has traveled the world," says Zack Snyder. "Henry comes from a military family, and has a sense of duty." In Snyder's view, these elements helped give Cavill a sincerity that few others could pull off.

"We were always aware of Henry," recalls Charles Roven. "He had been the finalist in a previous attempt to do a Superman film, and he retained his desire to play the Man of Steel. But we did a thorough discovery, and not only the known actors. [Casting directors] Kristy Carlson and Lora Kennedy were involved in an exhaustive international reading and testing program. We wanted to be sure we didn't leave any stone unturned, because we knew if we wanted the movie to be as good as it could possibly be, we couldn't make a casting mistake. Henry always rose to the top, to the point where we finally did a film test with him. And he just knocked it out of the park."

After winning the role, Cavill read up on Superman comics to gain a sense of the character's history and establish a baseline on which to build his own interpretation. "He's far more complex than people think," he says. "He's not just this perfect character. He's an incredibly conflicted and lonely and lost person."

Christopher Nolan sees in Henry Cavill the same qualities that attracted audiences to Christopher Reeve, whose portrayal in 1978's *Superman: The Movie* made him a hero of Nolan's childhood. "[Henry] owns the part," he says. "It was extraordinary to watch his first test, and then seeing the film and what he did with it. It's a very powerful portrayal, the way he conveys the strength and dignity of Superman. He rises to that challenge. And he's also Clark, relatable and vulnerable—somewhat ironically, for an alien."

As Clark Kent, Superman grows up in the rural environment of Smallville, Kansas, frustrated by having to prevent himself from lashing out at the peers who harass him. "I think any kid who's been bullied feels that way," Cavill says. "But it's just amplified by the fact that he really is powerless to do anything about it, while having all the power to do *everything* about it."

This quality of embodying two attitudes and two physical states at once is key to the Clark Kent/Superman dynamic. "He can fly—but he has to pretend that he can't," says Zack Snyder. Many actors can fill out a Super Hero's costume with a magazine idol's figure, but only Cavill nailed the sense of holding his immeasurable power in check at all times.

PAGES 32–33: Henry Cavill as Superman and Russell Crowe as Jor-El look out on Earth

BREAKING THE BODY'S LIMITS

So how did Henry Cavill become a literal Man of Steel? Working under lead fitness trainer Mark Twight, Cavill and other cast members drove themselves through a punishing regimen of power lifting, calisthenics, controlled-calorie dieting—and zero tolerance for shortcuts.

Twight is the founder of Gym Jones, a private Salt Lake City gym that preaches functional fitness over the mere *appearance* of fitness. A maxim on the gym's website reads: *Capacity strengthens confidence. A façade is merely physical.*

"Superman learned he could fly; I learned I could do things in the gym that I never thought possible," says Cavill. "It hurts. It's excruciating. But I enjoy pushing past that point. And once you've beaten yourself, in that your brain is telling you to stop and you force that little voice back, you realize your body's actually more than capable of doing it."

Twight's gym caters to elite fitness buffs, not dilettantes, with members including professional athletes and soldiers belonging to military special ops squads. Twight agrees to work with Hollywood types only if they agree to work just as hard in return.

On Zack Snyder's film *300*, Twight whipped an army of stunt men and actors into lean, fighting Spartans. For *Man of Steel*, Henry Cavill, Michael Shannon, Russell Crowe, and Antje Traue underwent Twight's program. Snyder sees the transformation that occurs behind the eyes, not only in the abs and biceps.

"When they train their bodies, they're experiencing a physical manifestation of their character," Snyder says. "The pain, the goals, the failures, the successes. All those things are like this mini crucible that they go through, and then come out the other side these other people. When we were doing *300*, you could see the actors who made the workout part of their acting. That's when it's not for vanity. The reward of the suffering is evident."

And even though he spends his time behind the camera, Snyder trained alongside his stars as often as he could, building up his stamina in preparation for the ordeal of making a film. "It's like a marathon—you train beforehand and you deplete over time," he says. "You have to get your strength together before you shoot, and see if you can make it to the end."

OPPOSITE: When a scene required Henry Cavill to go shirtless, it provided extra incentive for achieving physical perfection.

LEFT AND ABOVE: Henry Cavill found that physical training improved both body and mind.

MICHAEL SHANNON ➲ GENERAL ZOD

Michael Shannon plays General Zod, *Man of Steel*'s chief antagonist. Leader of Krypton's Warrior Guild, Zod is a would-be revolutionary who learned to value scientific discovery as one of Jor-El's closest friends.

On *Man of Steel*, Shannon channeled Zod's formidable strength through his words and actions, convinced that there was a degree of rightness behind the character's cause.

"I'm not a Kryptonian," he points out. "But if Earth was in such dire straits as Krypton, what side would you take? How would you feel about it? What would you try to do to stop it from happening? There are some people, like Jor-El, that try and deal with these circumstances in a scientific, compassionate manner. And there are some people that deal with it by force."

As Christopher Nolan and David Goyer developed the *Man of Steel* story, they established the class structures of Krypton and the societal pressures that would drive men like Zod to mutiny. "We talked a lot about Krypton as a dying civilization," he says. "There are reasons why Krypton has failed. They

have a controlled population, and a caste system that has developed." Although Zod sees value in the programmed roles of Krypton's castes, he has no patience for the outmoded constraints of the Kryptonian Ruling Council.

Debbie Snyder sees the rationality behind Zod's ruthlessness, pointing out that a sneering villain would have felt empty and false. "Zod's not wrong," she says. "If the shoe's on the other foot, if you had the chance to save your entire people, you'd have to take it. When you're playing for keeps, when it's the end of your race, there are no rules."

Like Jor-El, Zod hopes to initiate the rebirth of his dying world. However, Jor-El knew Krypton's case was terminal and sent his only son to Earth in an act of hope. Zod was blindsided by the planet's destruction and has no sentimental attachment to the earthlings he discovers. If billions of humans need to die to make Earth into a new Krypton, he's comfortable with the collateral damage.

Debbie Snyder also points out an interesting wrinkle in the relationship between Zod and Clark Kent, whom Zod would have called Kal-El. "In their culture, [Zod] could have raised Clark,"

TOP: Michael Shannon holds Zod's fury in check.

LEFT: Zod's menacing gaze conveys power without words.

OPPOSITE: When Zod is exposed to the unique radiation of Earth's sun, his eyes become deadly weapons.

she says, referring to the familial traditions of Krypton that took shape during the film's conceptual world-building. "If you defeat an adversary in battle, and they have a child, you would raise them. It was the honorable thing to do. So there are layers."

Shannon has a grip on Zod's ironclad authority, speaking with a gravity that makes his ultimatum to Superman a tough offer to refuse. "When he's on set and he's in the moment, he is so intense," says Debbie Snyder. "And then he finishes the scene, and all of a sudden he cracks a joke. And you're like, 'Oh I forgot, he's a nice guy.'"

Adds Christopher Nolan, "Michael was able to carry a layer of tragedy to define a sense of purpose to the character."

Because Zod is the head of Krypton's military, it's likely that he distinguished himself many times on the battlefield prior to his ultimate betrayal of the Kryptonian Council. Fittingly, his armor is the most intimidating outfit worn by any character in the film, made of sizable, angular modules that form an interlocking shield. The armor is too bulky, in fact, to be realized by anything other than CG.

"This [armor] is created by technology that we can't understand, so they would not be limited by movements that we would imagine," explains Zack Snyder. Had Shannon worn a physical costume with machined pieces fixed in place, he would have needed to shuffle around set like an overburdened gladiator. Instead, he wore a simple unitard marked with reference guidelines for later use by the visual effects crew.

Explains costume designer Michael Wilkinson, "Because the shapes were so big, they were extremely complex, and were hard planes that stole away from his body. We decided to render all of that armor digitally. I designed and drew with my illustrators the front and back views of the armor, and then handed them over to the visual effects team. They created it in 3-D and snapped it onto the body digitally."

As seen in concept art, Zod's armor bristles with weapons, including a sidearm in a leg holster and a gauntlet-mounted bayonet. "On Krypton, they're a warring culture and they don't have superpowers," Zack Snyder points out. "They just duke it out with each other. We wanted to include elements of a martial culture within that design."

For Zod, his combination of unshakable resolve and a fearsome suit of armor prepares him for battle both inside and out. And he'll need it, when faced with the challenge of recruiting Kal-El and restoring his vanished planet.

THESE PAGES: Zod and Faora wear the battle armor of the Kryptonian Warrior Guild.

THESE PAGES: A variety of designs depicting General Zod's battle armor. His bulky coverings are intimidating and dehumanizing.

AMY ADAMS ● LOIS LANE

Lois Lane is one of the most prominent female characters in fiction, and actresses have interpreted her role for decades. This didn't intimidate Amy Adams one bit, though. "I come from theater, so roles are constantly redone," she says. "It never throws me to have to reimagine a role or to come at it from a new point of view. To me it's very exciting."

"Amy is a joy to work with in every way," says Zack Snyder. "She can do anything, she can sing and dance—not that I asked her to do that—and she's an amazing actor." Debbie Snyder agrees, praising Adams's ability to pivot from a serious film like *The Master* into entertaining fare like *The Muppets*: "She's feisty and smart, and what she brought to Lois is strength, beauty, and emotion. She embodies the best of all of us."

The Superman legend just doesn't work without Lois Lane, who was already Clark Kent's smarter, gutsier newsroom rival when the Man of Steel made his debut in *Action Comics* #1 in 1938. "She was a really ballsy reporter and was out doing her thing," says Debbie Snyder. "She was working in a time when not that many women had those high-powered jobs."

The creators of *Man of Steel* approached the character with a full understanding of her tendency to barrel into danger without caring about the consequences. In the screenplay, her background as a Pulitzer Prize–winning journalist is filled out with a mention of her stint as an embedded reporter with the First Infantry Division of the U.S. Army.

"One thing I am so proud of in this film is that Lois is such a strong female character and she's not just this damsel in distress," says Debbie Snyder. "Although [Superman] saves her physically, she saves him emotionally. And she has a very big part in the plan to overtake the bad guys. She's not just waiting for someone else. I like seeing these strong female characters, and I think that Zack always has strong female characters in his films."

Adams saw a lot to like about Lois's straightforward approachability, a quality that would appeal to a Kansas farm boy. "I think there was a great juxtaposition between this sort of Man of Steel and woman of Earth," she says. "Lois is just very natural, nothing about her is contrived or manufactured. She probably eats on the run, and eats a lot of room service, and she's not in the gym worrying about her figure."

Debbie Snyder adds that, while Lois and Superman immediately click, their upbringings are on opposite ends of a cultural gulf that makes their romance like the pairing of a

ABOVE: Amy Adams as the unstoppable *Daily Planet* reporter Lois Lane.

OPPOSITE: Costuming choices for Lois's travel ensemble emphasized low-key practicality.

country mouse with a city mouse. "The fact that he picks Lois makes him better," she says. "Because Lois is not the obvious choice. She's difficult, she's sophisticated, she's from the city, she's all the things that he's not. They make a really interesting couple, but a complicated couple."

For Lois's costumes, Michael Wilkinson saw the value in keeping things simple. "We tried to do things that were very strong and realistic, and not overly glamorize anything," he says. "We [gave] her a believable and strong silhouette that seemed to match her character."

Adds Henry Cavill, "I think the interaction between [Lois] and Superman is that she is obviously superwoman, in a societal sense. And then she's finally found this one guy who can literally sweep her off her feet."

RUSSELL CROWE ✧ JOR-EL

Jor-El is Superman's biological father, but moviegoers familiar with the character are likely to remember Marlon Brando's star turn as Jor-El in 1978's *Superman: The Movie*. But Brando's role was a mere cameo compared to the major screen time and demanding physical shoot required to realize the character in *Man of Steel*. While this new version of Jor-El is very different from Brando's in a number of ways, the character was portrayed by an actor with comparable gravitas.

"There is a touch of madness to Jor-El," says Crowe. "There's a touch of insanity in what he's doing; massive desperation. As far as he's concerned, it's the last throw of the dice for the entire race."

"Russell's character sacrificed his life for Clark," Debbie Snyder points out. "He could have come with him, but he knew that for Clark to truly have a choice he had to leave the rest of the old world behind." Zack Snyder adds to the thought, explaining that Jor-El realized the importance of cutting ties, even though the act required him and his wife Lara to die: "They're Kryptonians, they're tied to Krypton. All the decisions they make are influenced by that fact. There's no way they could have raised Kal on Earth objectively. They had to let him go and be raised apart, so that one day when he had to make a choice, they would not have influenced that decision in any way."

TOP: Russell Crowe as Jor-El wearing his Kryptonian battle armor.
LEFT: This costume design for Jor-El combines the regal finery of Krypton's ruling caste with the simple colors and clean lines used by the House of El.
OPPOSITE: A concept illustration depicting Jor-El's flying mount, the war kite named H'raka.

Costume designer Michael Wilkinson thought of Jor-El as the iconoclast among the Kryptonian traditionalists and went with a muted look for the character's outfits when compared to the sartorial choices of his peers. "We kind of liked the idea of him being quite simple in his clothes, among the sort of crazy-elaborate nature of the rest of the Kryptonian costumes," he says. But transforming this design into Russell Crowe's actual outfit raised new challenges for Wilkinson, particularly during the week-long filming of an underwater sequence set in Krypton's "Genesis Chamber." Wilkinson discovered that the subaquatic lighting turned Jor-El's suit into such a vibrant blue that it seemed as if the character had made a sudden costume change.

As General Zod, Michael Shannon knew his character was an old friend of Jor-El's, and that their confrontation would be a heartbreaking clash of Cain and Abel. Yet Shannon is a decade younger than Crowe, and he viewed the older actor as someone who existed on a higher tier. "He's got more experience than I have, and I kept trying to wrap my head around how to be his

equal," he says. "I think in the end we decided that, in a way, he was kind of a mentor to Zod. That maybe he was not exactly the same generation."

Crowe immediately saw the connection between Jor-El and Zod, and viewed the two as more alike than not. "Zod has a concept too, in terms of keeping Krypton alive," he says. "I think that's where the two of them agree, that by whatever means necessary you have to propagate the race. It's a pretty heavy series of decisions to make, [and] I'm not sure that Jor-El is in any way really a good man. I think they're both working under extreme pressure and a period of desperation. They both make the decisions that appear to be right under those pressures."

Antje Traue, who plays Zod's loyal "Sub Commander" Faora, could feel a charge in the air every time Crowe stepped on set. "He's like a magnet," she says. "When he steps into a room, everybody becomes very quiet. There's just a lot of respect, and we all know why."

PAGES 48-49: After a perilous underwater journey, Jor-El emerges in the heart of the Genesis Chamber. Its inner walls seem to be lined with active neurons, a fitting choice for the place that is the nerve center of Kryptonian population control.

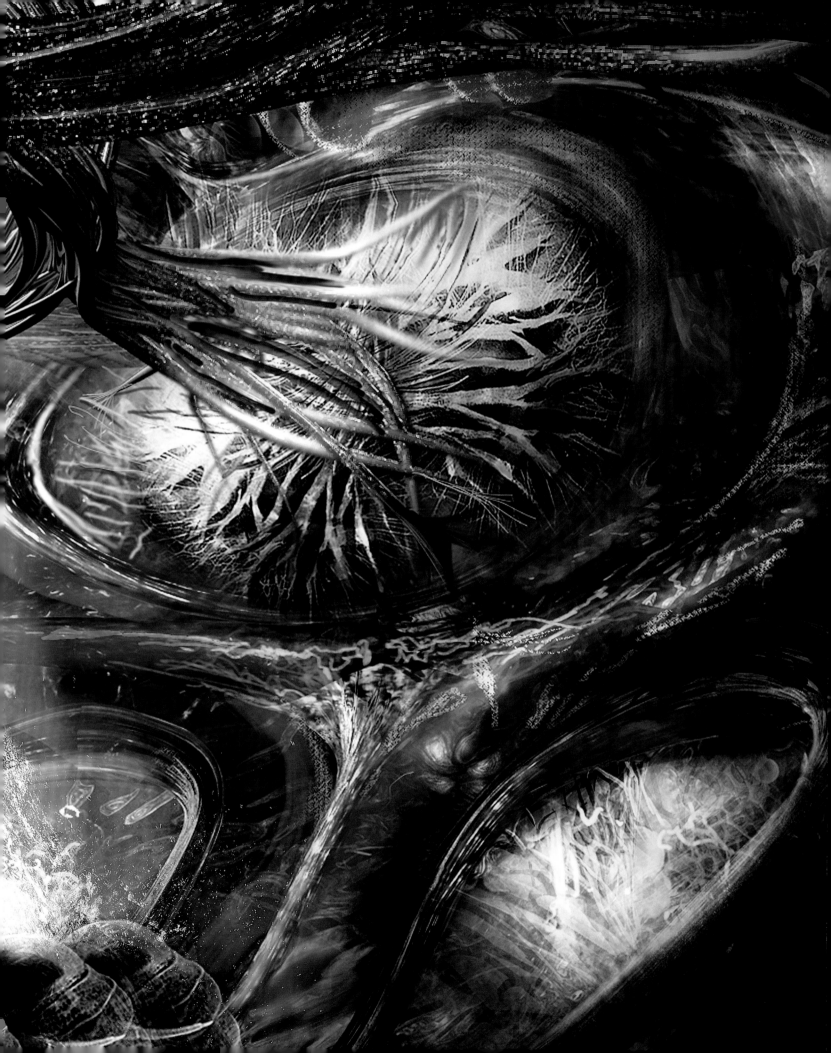

KEVIN COSTNER ★ JONATHAN KENT

Kevin Costner is also a father in *Man of Steel*, but he plays a very different man than the alien scientist Jor-El. Jonathan Kent is an unpretentious Kansas farmer who adopts an alien boy and loves him as his own.

"Every son feels like maybe he wants to take his dad on," says Costner, noting that there is something universal in the way that Clark seeks to outgrow Jonathan's sheltering presence. "But by the time a son is actually physically capable of doing that, they don't want to anymore. All that's left is a love and respect."

Debbie Snyder marvels at Costner's practical approach. "Kevin is just amazingly down-to-earth," she says. "He's just trying to get by and teach his son right from wrong in a world that's not always kind. He doesn't know where his son came from. There's a lot of unanswered questions, and he's trying to do the best he can. In so many ways he's the heart of the film; who he is and what he taught Clark resonates throughout."

Costner and Diane Lane form a family unit to keep their adopted son morally and culturally grounded. That doesn't mean they understand exactly what Clark is going through, as he manifests super-senses that aren't covered in any parenting guidebook. But, like parents everywhere, they try to set the best example they can for the child who will one day carry on their name.

"They're afraid that someone, once they know who he is, will take [Clark] away," says Debbie Snyder. Zack Snyder expands upon the worry that forever haunted the Kents: "The Russians, or the aliens, or the government, they could somehow take Clark away from them once they found out what he could do." When that moment ultimately arrives, the Kansas values of Jonathan and Martha Kent may ultimately decide Earth's fate.

"Martha and Jonathan take human culture to a stylized perfection," adds Zack Snyder. "They live honestly off the land; their morality is shaped by their relationship to their community. They're honest, hardworking people. That power is the ultimate morality that shapes the universe."

DIANE LANE ★ MARTHA KENT

Diane Lane plays Martha Kent, the woman who raises an otherworldly child and teaches him that emotional bonds are stronger than genetic ones.

Martha Kent isn't a perfect woman, but she is open and honest, with a practical approach to dealing with a truly unique parenting challenge. Lane believes that Martha is, above all else, a pragmatist: "I think she has to be, because when you find this star child in your barn and realize all the capacities that this young being has, there's a moral obligation to be the best tour guide you can be. That's how I approach motherhood, and I think that that's what it winds up being: You explain the world you are born into the best you can."

Flashback scenes in *Man of Steel* illustrate how Martha handles Clark's extraordinary needs, and with the stakes so high it's inevitable that she is held to a higher standard. "There's a lot of explaining to do, as a parent, when you're saying, 'do this, not that, [and] trust us,'" Lane says. "But when somebody can hear everything you say and see through walls? You must live a life with no hypocrisy, and walk that line as a parent more than most."

As an adoptive mother, Martha Kent provides a quality that's a foreign concept on Krypton: unconditional love. Lane infuses her character with the wisdom and courage to face an unprecedented test. "You definitely feel chosen with this golden opportunity," she says. "What are you going to do with this potentiality of a person?"

OPPOSITE BOTTOM LEFT: Kevin Costner's Jonathan Kent passes on down-to-earth advice to his adopted teenage son Clark, played by Dylan Sprayberry.

OPPOSITE RIGHT: Costuming for Kevin Costner's Jonathan Kent emphasized sensible work clothes that would appeal to a hardworking farmer.

TOP: Diane Lane filmed several flashback scenes that required her to portray Martha Clark at multiple life stages.

LEFT, ABOVE, AND OPPOSITE BOTTOM: Lara's costumes are simpler than those of many Kryptonians and emphasize natural materials.

OPPOSITE TOP: Ayelet Zurer infused her scenes alongside Russell Crowe with bittersweet love and a sense of impending tragedy.

PAGES 54–55: Lara Lor-Van watches the death of her world, secure in the knowledge that she has given her son a new beginning.

AYELET ZURER 🜨 LARA LOR-VAN

Ayelet Zurer is Superman's birth mother, Lara Lor-Van. In *Man of Steel*, Lara is the first Kryptonian to become pregnant and give birth naturally in countless generations. This is a declaration of revolution on Krypton, where what should be a quiet, sacred act has been criminalized by a people who have drifted too far from their roots. By letting her child escape into the universe while she remains behind on a doomed world, Lara makes the ultimate sacrifice for her son and for the future of her people.

"It's funny; it's like we're playing people from another planet, but actually we are playing the metaphor for the core of human life," says Zurer. In the film's themes, she sees the echo of a quote attributed to political crusader Nelson Mandela: *Our worst fear is not that we are inadequate; our deepest fear is that we are powerful beyond measure.* "This is the essence of it," she says.

Lara shares the radical values of her husband, Jor-El, and her costumes follow a similar aesthetic. While recognizably alien, they aren't nearly as stifling or as decadent as those worn by the members of the Kryptonian Council. "When I first met Zack, we talked about a movie that we both liked and watched when we were kids," she says. "It was *Excalibur*. So that was my reference to the time and the texture [of Krypton]. The clothing, the hair, the makeup. That earthy, thick, very heavy, and dark time."

Lara Lor-Van, who gives up everything so that Krypton might survive through her son, is the clearest example of why the *S* insignia that Superman wears on his chest is the Kryptonian symbol of hope.

53

THIS PAGE: Antje Traue as Faora gives a frosty glare as she stands in front of the inscribed heat shield of Kal-El's space capsule.

OPPOSITE TOP: Concept art shows Faora inside a full-body space suit used in the exploration of long-dead Kryptonian colonies.

OPPOSITE BOTTOM: Traue in the Kryptonian Council Chamber, wearing a particularly ornate set of armor.

ANTJE TRAUE ✍ FAORA

Antje Traue relished the chance to play Sub-Commander Faora, the piti-less killer who is described in the screenplay as the "tigress of Zod." As Faora, Traue exudes an ice-cold edge and moves with the precision of a surgeon's scalpel.

"Violence is her satisfaction," says Traue, who saw Faora as a genetic automaton unburdened by either mercy or a sense of fair play. "I thought there should be no subtext, no double meaning for her. This is what she is. She's trained to attack good men, just to protect her Krypton."

"We were looking for an international presence, because we wanted the character of Faora to not feel American," recalls Charles Roven. "We did a true multi-geographical search and Antje was the fruit of that labor."

In preparing for the role, Traue strove to become socially unattached. "I isolated myself," she says. "I really was focused on the physical training and my own discipline." Only one crack in Faora's armor is ever shown on screen, and this small show of emotion is triggered by nothing less than the annihilation of her homeworld. "It was kind of a relief actually, to let that shell go, and to give her that moment of vulnerability," she says.

Traue spent hours pushing her body to the limits, under the conviction that her sweat would pay off in her character's authenticity. "I wanted to feel Faora's powers and not just imagine them," she says. "And working out and lifting weights made me experience that there's beauty to physical strength, and fearlessness, and power."

That level of dedication is what you'd expect from Faora, who remains icily committed to the ideals espoused by Zod and who never questions her orders. When confronted with such an implacable adversary, Earth faces a dire threat.

ZOD'S INSURGENTS

They call themselves the Sword of Rao. General Zod's followers are handpicked loyalists from the Warrior Guild, sworn to overthrow the Council and sever the degenerative bloodlines that weaken Krypton. The Council members are the ones who rule Krypton, and who have allowed their world to deteriorate from apathy. Zod's insurgents are easily whipped into a fanatic frenzy, and are willing to take on the Council members even though it means battling the elite Sapphire Guard. But their dream of life under Zod's rule is shattered by a sentence of imprisonment in the alternate dimension called the Phantom Zone.

Jax-Ur is the cadaverous chief scientist among Zod's crew. He hungers for knowledge, whatever the cost, and is above ethical concerns regarding torture and medical experimentation. On Krypton, Jax-Ur served as a geneticist within the Science Guild, where his skills helped shape the hereditary destinies of every citizen grown inside optimized, artificial embryos.

Nam-Ek is an impossible hulk of a being, whose muscled form is imposing even when he's dressed in his skinsuit—and who becomes downright terrifying when he armors up. Because all Zod's Kryptonians receive superpowers upon their arrival on Earth, the pumped-up Nam-Ek seems like the living embodiment of overkill. The screenplay describes him as silent, a quality that lets his actions do the talking. Nine feet tall, Nam-Ek received genetic programming to give him the ideal traits of an obedient and uncompromising soldier. Nam-Ek is a member of the Warrior Guild and is incapable of leadership, responding only to the orders of his superiors.

OPPOSITE LEFT: Utterly unscrupulous scientist Jax-Ur played by actor Mackenzie Gray.

OPPOSITE RIGHT: Concept art depicts two more of Zod's insurgents, Nadira, played in *Man of Steel* by Apollonia Vanova, and Dev-Em, who was portrayed by Revard Dufresne.

ABOVE: Towering over nine feet tall, the formidable Nam-Ek unleashes destruction on the streets of Smallville.

LEFT: Zod's warriors are equipped with formidable battle armor.

LAURENCE FISHBURNE ● PERRY WHITE

Perry White is the no-nonsense editor in chief of the *Daily Planet*, and right from the start the *Man of Steel* team knew he had to be more than a caricature. "We didn't want him to be a cliché in terms of what you would think of as the head of a newspaper," says Debbie Snyder.

Enter Laurence Fishburne, a longtime Superman fan who based his portrayal on the late Ed Bradley, a fixture of the CBS news program *60 Minutes*. "I would often see Ed in New Orleans," remembers Fishburne, whose love of music let him rub elbows with Bradley at the New Orleans Jazz Fest. "He was a guy who was a great interviewer; he was a great thinker; he was a guy from humble beginnings."

When Fishburne joined the cast, Zack Snyder felt that his team had pulled off a minor coup. "He's immensely talented," he says. "I've always been a huge fan of his, and he brings his stature to this iconic role. He makes it better and stronger in every moment."

In *Man of Steel*, Metropolis is hit by the perfect storm of an alien superweapon and a Kryptonian invasion. When Perry's assistant Jenny is trapped beneath the rubble, Perry rallies his own troops to perform heroism on a mortal scale. "We're sort of left to try to help her out of it, and we have to risk our lives to do that," Fishburne says. "[It's] that sort of Superman/Everyman thing. We have to step up and do something that we don't think we can do."

Viewers don't meet Lois Lane's mother and father in *Man of Steel*, but that doesn't mean she lacks an on-screen family. Amy Adams eagerly endorses Fishburne's Perry White and the actors who play the office staffers and reporters from the newspaper bullpen. "It felt like I've known them for a really long time. Just immediately, I felt a warmth and a rapport," she says. "The *Daily Planet* stuff, I had a blast because I feel like that's where Lois is the most comfortable. That's where she feels the most powerful, that's her world."

Adds Debbie Snyder, "I think in the world of journalism, who knows where you're going to end up. You're in the middle of conflict. And I feel that the *Daily Planet*, they're family. They spend a lot of time in there, but they've also been in dangerous situations together."

Fishburne views Perry White both as a mentor and as someone who paid his dues chasing down stories. He understands what makes Lois Lane tick, and he probably knows her better than anyone in *Man of Steel*. "Perry has a history of being a reporter and doing these kinds of investigations himself, so he knows from the inside what she must be feeling," he says, putting into perspective Lois's tenacity in her pursuit of the big Superman story. "She's got this piece of information, she's made this huge discovery, and she can't really reveal all that she knows."

TOP: Laurence Fishburne as Perry White oozes calm competence, even when faced with carnage in Metropolis. Actor Michael Kelly, who plays Steve Lombard, is at his side.

RICHARD SCHIFF — DR. EMIL HAMILTON

A supporting character in the Superman comics, Dr. Emil Hamilton is a brilliant scientist who has decided to use his smarts for the benefit of humanity. Richard Schiff adds a dash of humor to the disciplined ranks of the military personnel mobilized to respond to an emerging alien threat.

"He's probably somebody who is so fascinated with the technology and the science, and that maybe gets him a little too wrapped up," Schiff says. "I think he's a techno freak and a physics freak and somebody who is just amazed by what these people from another planet can achieve."

Dr. Hamilton comes packaged with the rest of the military's forces, but he holds no rank and brings the outsider's perspective of a civilian: "While they're getting into battle mode, I'm like, 'Holy cow, look at that!' I think he's just fascinated with the science of it."

CHRISTOPHER MELONI — COLONEL HARDY

When General Zod's Kryptonians menace our planet, the people of Earth aren't about to take it lying down. Christopher Meloni plays Colonel Hardy, a hard-bitten military officer attached to U.S. Northcom. "Chris Meloni had the most complex schedule to work out, because of his television show," recalls producer Charles Roven. "But he really wanted to make the film with us, and he really wanted to play the character. We had to carefully carve out specific times for him to work so we didn't tie him up for the whole schedule."

Roven is quick to praise Meloni's ability to effortlessly capture the essence of military readiness: "He's a perfect guy for it. He can be tough, he can be strong, he's got terrific one-liners, and he's the guy you want out there when you need some backup. He's the guy you want behind you if you're in an alley and you run into some tough aliens from Krypton."

For his part, Meloni was happy to have the chance to exchange notes with actual soldiers in uniform during the preparation and filming of his scenes. "I've shot some guns," he says, "but we had to go through all these tactics of movement. Where the targets are, how you have to go after them, and priorities on the battlefield. It was pretty cool."

THIS PAGE: The incredible ensemble cast of *Man of Steel* brought a sense of realism to Superman's world.

HARRY LENNIX — GENERAL SWANWICK

Harry Lennix's ability to project an aura of strength and authority made him a perfect fit for the role of General Swanwick in *Man of Steel*.

In the film Swanwick heads the joint military operations of United States Northern Command, or U.S. Northcom. His position comes with power, and Swanwick can't afford to take any threat lightly. As events unfold and he's forced to confront the reality of a living weapon like Superman, it is Lennix's thoughtful portrayal that treads the line between caution and trust.

FORGET STRAIGHT LINES and brushed metal surfaces. Those clichés of sci-fi futurism are nowhere to be found on *Man of Steel*'s Krypton, but that doesn't make the world any less alien. Krypton is a setting both frighteningly advanced and impossibly ancient, formed from windswept curves and crawling with intricate tendrils.

"In reinventing Superman I think you have to start from the very beginning and re-educate everybody," says Debbie Snyder. "We can't assume that everyone knows the story. [Understanding] Krypton is necessary to get an understanding of the sacrifices everybody made, of how special Clark was, to know the culture where he came from."

For co-producer Wes Coller, Krypton is a character in its own right. "Early on we realized that Krypton was going to play a much bigger role than just being an environment that part of the film takes place in," he says. That meant a lot of work went into "casting" Krypton through design and visual stylization.

But *design* is too tame a word for the Krypton of *Man of Steel*. This environment was the product of *world-building*: the melding of motifs, narratives, and fictional backstories into a coherent and lived-in setting. "Every minute detail [of Krypton] has been planned out to make sense," says Debbie Snyder. "Their technology, their power, their ships, their weapons."

It started with a story. Writer David Goyer hammered out Krypton's history as he developed the screenplay, envisioning a society so connected with nature that it eventually overreached and killed the very thing that it loved. "Krypton is a world that has completely exhausted its natural resources," he explains. "Krypton is kind of an ecological cautionary tale. It's a very rigid society, and hopefully, at least for earthlings, it's not a world we would particularly love to live on."

Zack Snyder throws the issue into sharp relief: "The dirt of Krypton and the flesh of the Kryptonians are the same. The Kryptonians and their planet are tied together, and they have caused the destruction of their world by harvesting the core of their planet for energy. The path that the Kryptonians take, morally, mirrors the path that their planet has taken. As a society they turned away from space travel and became isolated. They started trying to control their population and took love out of their society. That led to their downfall."

Story beats and cultural nuances came to visual life through the efforts of the art department under the guidance of production designer Alex McDowell. "What's really evident on a film like this," he says, "is how important it is to think about story not in a linear, script-driven way, but in a world-building way, where you can start by developing the logic of the backstory from the current storytelling, extrapolating back from that into the deep history. It begins to give an underlying coherence to all the parts in the film, everything from the environments to the props to the robots to the characters."

McDowell emphasizes greed as the prime shaper of Krypton's environment, as the people dug deep in pursuit of the plasma at the planet's heart. "This is a world that may once have been lush, but its energy, its electricity, the basic power of the planet comes from deep in the core. And, in fact, the planet self-destructs because they've exploited the core of the planet, to the extent that it blows up."

World-building is laborious and intense, but Goyer is confident the payoff justifies the investment. "It takes a lot of time, but we're very thorough," he says. "Hopefully some of that will seep into what the actors are doing and it will make the audience have a much richer experience."

PAGES 62–63: Concept artwork of the Genesis Chamber portrays delicate strings of embryo sacs.

THESE PAGES: The surface of Krypton reveals the greedy extent of its resource mining, leaving behind a planetary crust that appears to be on the verge of crumbling.

KANDOR

Its surface is cut into ribbons, letting light filter through the slashes in the planetary crust to reach the subterranean habitats below. This is Kandor, the capital of Krypton and the home of the planet's Ruling Council. "It's like the planet itself has been carved into a city," explains Snyder, "which is something we wanted to say. Symbolically, they had gone too far."

Alex McDowell provides additional context to the iconic look of the capital: "A very conceptual idea we developed with one of the artists, Rick Buoen, was the idea that the whole surface of the planet's been strip-mined to the point where the planet's basically barren. And people have moved down from the outer surface into caves under the ground. The ground itself is carved into these furrows. The furrows became the recognizable landscape of Krypton, but they tell a deep story about exploitation."

OPPOSITE TOP: The windswept contours of Kandor are on display in this finished VFX shot from *Man of Steel*.

BELOW: An enormous defense cruiser makes a pass above the city of Kandor in this conceptual illustration.

PAGES 68–69: Illuminated at night, Krypton's capital city hums with activity.

THE COUNCIL CHAMBER

Looming above the half-buried city of Kandor is the governmental tower of Krypton's Ruling Council. Composed of representatives from all the planet's major guilds, the Council is weary, antiquated, and close to death. Its surroundings, however, still hold an air of grandeur despite the obvious odor of decay.

"The Council Chamber was, I think, the first building we really designed," says Alex McDowell. "It's the most ancient building in Krypton; it's the seat of power. As it evolved, it turned into something that had [an] animation component so it could open and close in the atmosphere."

The tower's central meeting room can unfold like a blossoming flower. Illuminated channels within the walls provide a breathtaking beauty that seems at odds with the Council's stubborn insistence on dead-end traditionalism.

"It's very old; it's really decayed," says McDowell of the Council Chamber, which upon close inspection reveals signs of neglect from its caretakers. "It's kind of dirty. It's become highly ritualized and formalized."

Pillars and walls within the chamber bear inscriptions of letters and glyphs, carved a quarter-inch deep into nearly every surface of the physical elements found on the filming set. Some etchings still glitter with remnants of gilt inlay. Every structure has a cracked and crumbled appearance, and the *Man of Steel* crew sanded and filed edges and faces to give the appearance of natural erosion. In the design of the chamber, McDowell cites the artistic influence of electron microscope photography and macro photography of plant specimens.

LEFT AND OPPOSITE: These illustrations of the Ruling Council's spire resemble budding stalks and polished obsidian carvings.

PAGES 72–73: The hollows on either side of the Councilors' thrones give the chamber's interior the appearance of a sunken-eyed face.

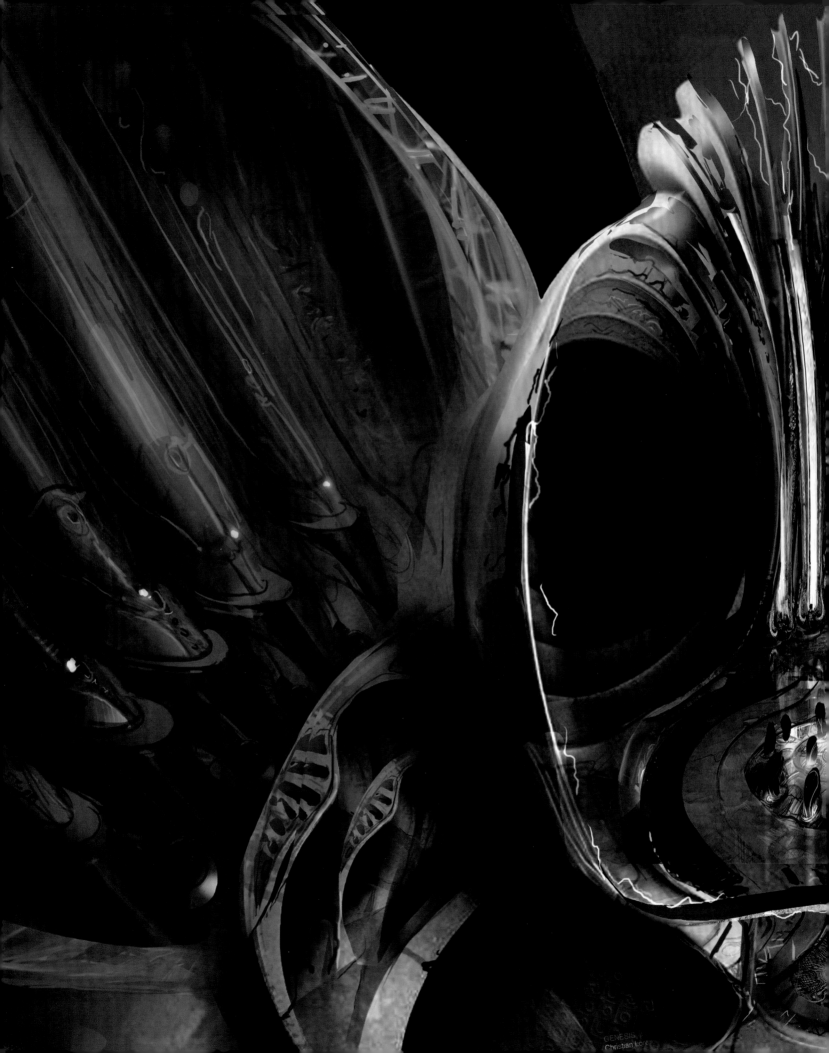

SPEAKING KRYPTONIAN

The Kryptonian language in the film is the work of Christine Schreyer, a linguistic anthropologist and assistant professor of anthropology at the University of British Columbia. Schreyer came aboard to consult on language creation and world-building during August 2011. Graphic designer Kirsten Franson then created the look of written Kryptonian, including an ornate ceremonial font and a utilitarian one used for labeling starship parts.

"My interest in created languages developed through an assignment I give my students to develop their own languages," says Schreyer. "Students usually find it hard to create a language without first imagining who the people are, and what their culture is like."

The first four phrases Schreyer developed appeared on the pillars of Krypton's Ruling Council Chamber: "These are my favorites, not only because they were the first sentences I developed, but also because the Council Chamber is a place where decisions are made about the future of the world and it is literally inscribed with Krypton's history." The phrases and their translations are:

The Light of Rao warms us.

The four Moons of Yuda protect us.

The Wisdom of Telle guides us.

The Beauty of Lorra inspires us.

Schreyer explains that another favorite was an in-joke, cooked up between Kirsten Franson and herself while working on words that would be printed on Kryptonian spacecraft: "We thought it would be funny to have a phrase that meant 'mind the gap' written near the edges of decks. The phrase literally means, 'your walking, think about (it).'"

Other phrases specifically developed for use on ships and weapons include:

Communications = literally "talking-place"

Maintenance = literally "fixing-place"

Observation = literally "seeing-place"

Navigation = literally "navigating-place"

Docking Port = literally "docking-place"

Kryptonian inscriptions are a mix of both functional and poetic language. Schreyer explains that Krypton's people etch phrases upon items that they hold dear, and each of these phrases holds an inspirational meaning.

Among the grammatical rules governing the Kryptonian language is a subject-object-verb sentence structure, different from the subject-verb-object cadence of English. The sentence "I see him" would be written in Kryptonian as "I him see." Says Schreyer, "We chose to use a subject-object-verb word order since people in Kryptonian society had become selfish to some extent, and saw themselves—the doers of the action—to be the most important. Objects, which have a long-inscribed history and are inherited from one generation to the next, were seen as the next most important thing, and finally the verbs or the action itself."

So could the Kryptonian language be mastered by a dedicated earthling? Schreyer thinks so, with a little help. "Someone who is good with languages would be able to notice patterns that are recurring, but unless they had a key that told them the sounds and meaning of each of the symbols, they likely wouldn't be able to understand the language," she says. "However, if an earthling met a Kryptonian, eventually they would be able to communicate with each other. Spoken Kryptonian is based on regular linguistics principles, and is intended to be a language that could be learned if motivated learners exist!"

OPPOSITE: Illumination is at the heart of this conceptual piece that depicts the sentencing of Zod's insurgents. Channels of light extend from the back of each Councilor's throne and up to the heavens.

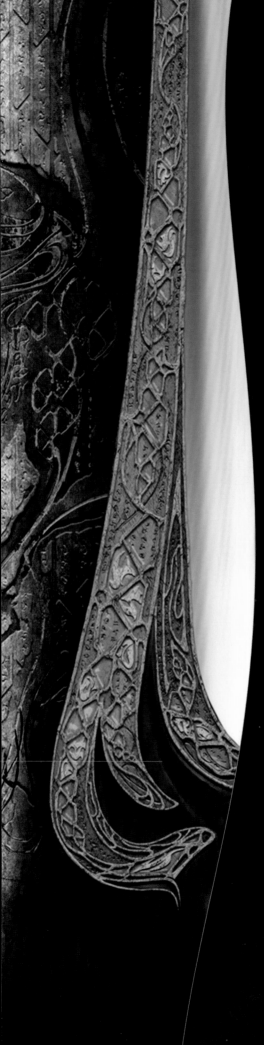

THE RULING COUNCIL

The Kryptonian Councilors themselves are even more decadent. "It was really important for the costumes of the Council to convey what those characters represent," explains costume designer Michael Wilkinson. "Small-mindedness [and] a sense of holding on to tradition and cultural restraints that prevent looking at new solutions to problems."

The costumes are dreadfully elaborate, with ornate headdresses and endless layers of stacked fabrics that evoke the indulgence of the Versailles aristocracy just before the French Revolution. "The fabrics that I chose were extremely heavy," says Wilkinson. "We created our own fabrics to try to convey the sense of alien textures that [would be unfamiliar] to mere earthlings like ourselves. We etched into velvets. We embroidered fabrics. We screen-printed over the top of fabrics to get raised textures."

One Council member holds a handcrafted staff, its head carved into nested, intricate shapes. The hooked outline calls to mind the bleached skull of a vulture.

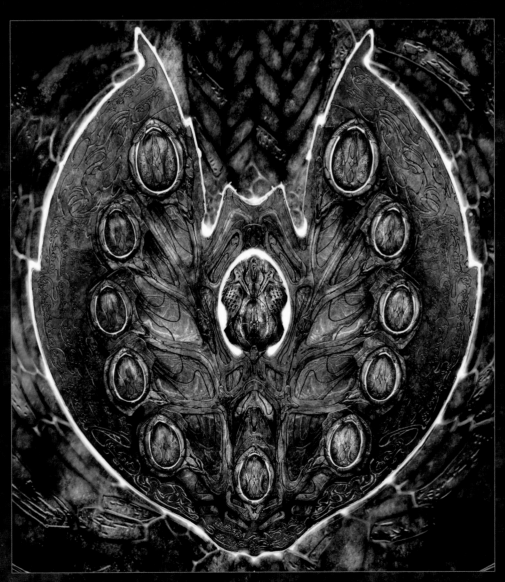

LEFT: The intricacy of Kryptonian carvings is on full view in this art piece, which also depicts the cracked finishes that indicate centuries of neglect. **ABOVE:** An overhead view of the platform on which Zod and his allies stand while being sentenced for their crimes. **PAGES 78–79:** This concept illustration highlights the faded elegance of the Kryptonian Council Chamber.

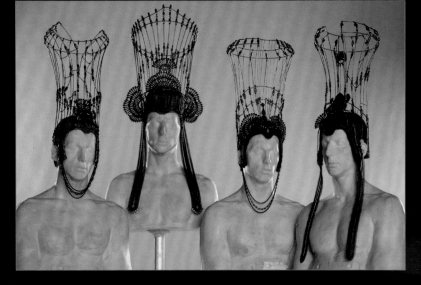

"It's a culture that was very sophisticated maybe a long time ago but sort of got mixed in their own small thinking and went into decline," explains Wilkinson. "With the costumes, we wanted them to feel like they were amazing five hundred years ago but have been over-encrusted and calcified by layers, and [they] haven't really had the resources to maintain them properly. So they just keep on getting heavier and more and more gritty, until we finally see them on the eve of their destruction in the film."

The Councilors, who speak for the castes of Krypton's stratified, genetically engineered society, bear chest glyphs similar to the *S* symbol of the House of El. The art department developed many such designs, which General Zod, his Sword of Rao insurgents, and members of the Council wear. Among the approved designs were glyphs representing the Warrior, Laborer, Thinker, Mediator, and Artisan guilds.

THESE PAGES: The costumes of the Kryptonian Ruling Council are simultaneously breathtaking and decadent. The intricate wirework around the head and shoulders suggests a crown, but also a cage.

CRAFTED TECHNOLOGY

There's no metal on Krypton. That decree was laid down during the early stages of world-building, forcing the designers to venture far afield and seek inspiration from anywhere except the obvious. If the energy-starved history of Krypton had eliminated the crutch of standard sci-fi designs, this new rule meant that artists couldn't fall back on suggesting high technology by including a touch of brushed steel or silvery chrome.

"We've sort of said that the planet is made of a combination of kind of bone marrow and insect shell," says Alex McDowell. "There's no rock or stone or metal."

Kryptonian prisoner manacles illustrate the point nicely. Because they couldn't look metallic, the art department instead designed the shackles to resemble the interlocked vertebrae of a slaughtered animal. General Zod's insurgents are locked into these when they receive their sentencing from the Council—appropriately wearing the bones of a dead thing before experiencing their own "living death" in the stasis of the Phantom Zone.

OPPOSITE: General Zod is secured in manacles that hug his spine, in imitation of his own vertebrae.

TOP: Car-Vex, played by Samantha Jo, awaits sentencing bound in unbreakable Kryptonian manacles.

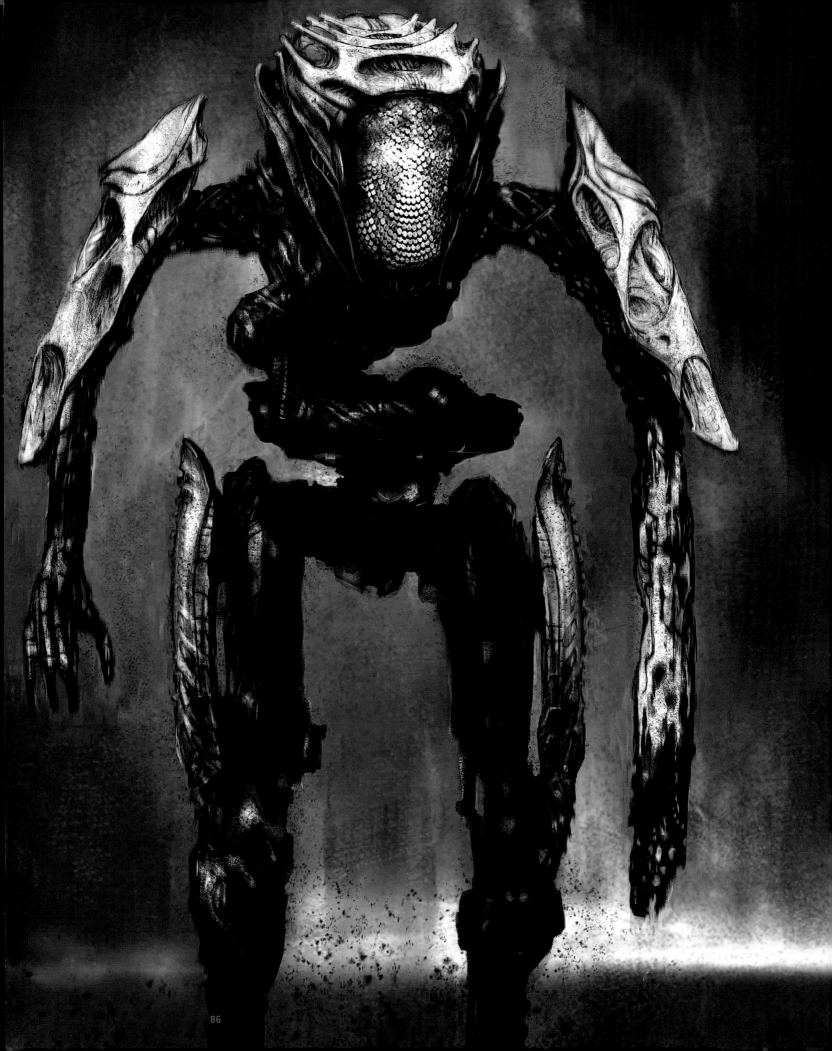

AUTOMATED HELPMATES

"This is an ancient planet whose history goes back so far they've actually gone beyond technology," says McDowell. "Their technology is vastly superior to ours, [but it] stopped for them twenty thousand years ago because they changed. Politically and socially they began to revert to a pre-technological state."

Nowhere is that more apparent than in the service robots that dote on their masters' needs like tireless clockwork butlers. There's almost nothing more sci-fi than a robot, and two of *Man of Steel*'s mechanical servants—Kelex and Kelor—have a history that dates from the Superman comics. But in *Man of Steel* they have nearly reached the end of their impossibly long operational lives.

"These robots are tens of thousands of years old," explains McDowell. "They are deeply imbued with character and history. And that idea of them being sort of ancient, carved objects is really interesting."

Kryptonian robots hover when in their default state, appearing as subtle, teardrop-shaped helpers subserviently awaiting further orders. Some models can transfigure into aggressive, humanoid configurations when their masters are threatened. The robots display information through the shifting, tactile screens that represent their faces.

Many variations on robot design came to life through concept art. One exhibited the ability to store small drones in a nested necklace configuration, deploying them one by one as bat-winged remotes.

PAGES 84–85: Jor-El and his faithful robot Kelex make their stand against those who would stop them.

OPPOSITE AND RIGHT: Kryptonian robots function as unobtrusive helpers unless pressed into battle.

BELOW: Kelex depicted in attack mode, fulfilling his role as guardian of the House of El.

THESE PAGES: Art concepts for Kryptonian robots experimented with humanoid and non-humanoid designs. The tentacled defender (opposite) is an aquabot, charged with maintaining the security of the Genesis Chamber.

ARMED FOR BATTLE

General Zod is evidence enough that Krypton boasts a warrior tradition. But because Kryptonians don't have superpowers under their red sun, they long ago perfected the killing arts through the production of plasma rifles and powered armor. When Zod, a lifelong soldier, discovers that Earth has turned his eyes into fiery weapons and his skin into armor, it is a revelation.

The Sapphire Guard is composed of ceremonial soldiers who stand watch over the Council Chamber and stop threats before they enter. Some pieces of early concept art generated for the Sapphire Guard were truly frightening, depicting armored hulks of almost unimaginable scale and proportions. Even an advanced and educated culture, the art seems to say, can be a brutal one.

Designs for the Council Chamber's Sapphire Guard members balanced functionality and tradition, in the manner of the sentries who stand at the gates of Buckingham Palace. A Guardsman uniform consists of sculpted armor pieces, a helmet, a cape, a staff, and a pair of inlaid gauntlets.

New Zealand's Weta Workshop made the film's Kryptonian props, including its rifles, carbines, and pistols. "The guns are a sort of microcosm of the primary materials," Alex McDowell points out. "So you have this lead-like material, you have this bone-like material, and then you have this kind of insect-shell hard material. And the guns themselves work on a kind of plasma energy."

ABOVE AND OPPOSITE TOP: Exploratory illustrations depict early iterations of the Kryptonian battle armor that would be seen in the finished film.

RIGHT: The members of the Sapphire Guard wear armor that evokes that worn by medieval knights.

OPPOSITE MIDDLE AND BOTTOM: Kryptonian weapons have an organic, bone-like feel.

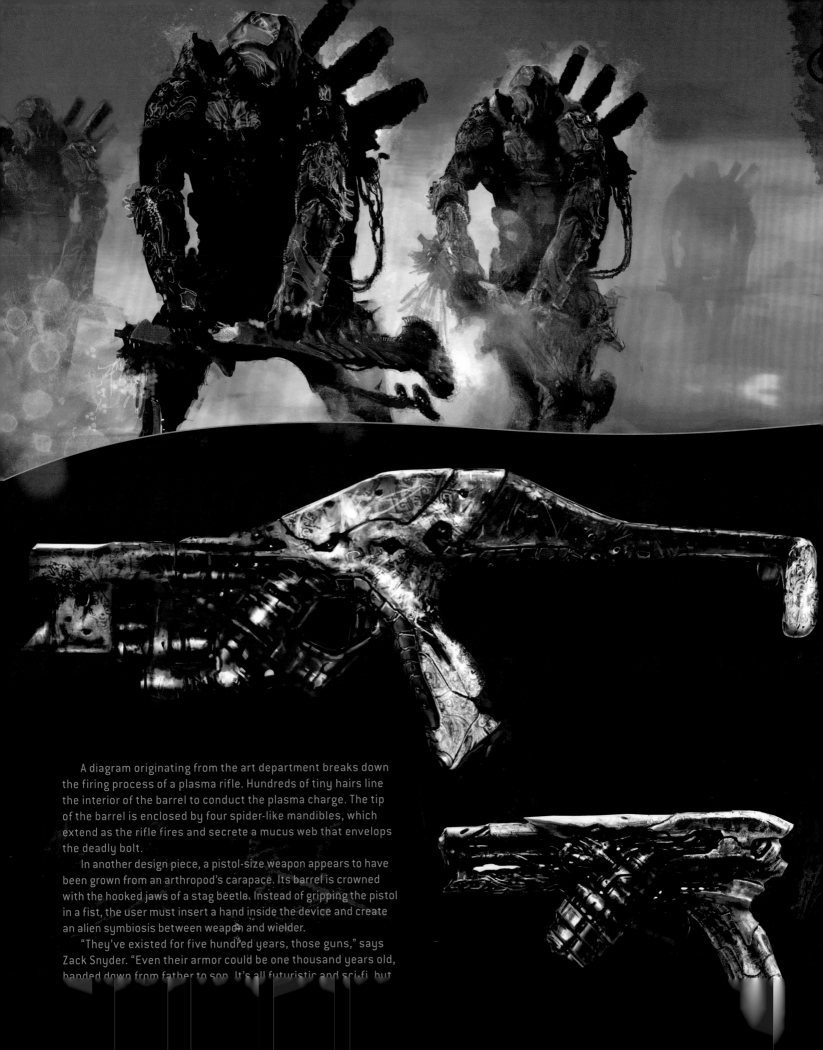

A diagram originating from the art department breaks down the firing process of a plasma rifle. Hundreds of tiny hairs line the interior of the barrel to conduct the plasma charge. The tip of the barrel is enclosed by four spider-like mandibles, which extend as the rifle fires and secrete a mucus web that envelops the deadly bolt.

In another design piece, a pistol-size weapon appears to have been grown from an arthropod's carapace. Its barrel is crowned with the hooked jaws of a stag beetle. Instead of gripping the pistol in a fist, the user must insert a hand inside the device and create an alien symbiosis between weapon and wielder.

"They've existed for five hundred years, those guns," says Zack Snyder. "Even their armor could be one thousand years old, handed down from father to son. It's all futuristic and sci-fi, but

THE HOUSE OF EL

From the cliff-top promontory that is his citadel, Jor-El can see everything—both the injured landscape stretched out beneath him and the glittering bowl of stars overhead. What better home for a scientist than an observatory?

Jor-El's decision to avoid Kandor's city center says a lot about his character, as does the citadel's integration within the crag itself. "All around are ruins," says Zack Snyder. "The implication is that once [the Kryptonians] had spread out, but now they've all retreated to the city. He's kind of on the outskirts."

Alex McDowell sees beauty in the House of El, citing the decision to make it an integral part of the surrounding topography and the use of biological motifs for the interior architecture. "It has that idea of being almost a grown object," he says. "It evolved from this tall tower into something more like an observatory on a mountaintop."

The quiet hallways inside seem to radiate peace and are inspired by the fractal curves found within a chambered nautilus.

"We ended up with this shell-like structure that hopefully looks like something that was almost grown out of the material itself rather than carved by sculptors," says McDowell. The art nouveau stylings of Superman's S insignia seem completely at home here. On one wall, the serpentine arcs of the familiar glyph aren't confined by a triangular border and instead trail away to become part of the structure itself.

"The House of El was completely practical," says Charles Roven. "The views outside the windows were CGI, but we built the house itself. We built the walls, the birthing bed, the science room. All the walls have the sophisticated Kryptonian language written on them, with proverbs and sayings."

"It actually is an almost completely physical environment that we've built," agrees McDowell, "created with a combination of computers, cut ribs, and boatbuilding technologies." Rapid

prototyping, in which 3-D computer modeling is used to help fabricate physical structures, is invaluable for a film on this scale. For the interiors of the House of El, computerized numerical control (CNC) was used to model the shapes of the ribs that provide the dwelling's architectural supports, and to then cut those shapes out of wood to produce full-size structures. "Huge wooden ribs, every single one unique, thousands of different shapes," says McDowell. "It would have taken months to print it out at full scale, lay it out on wood, and cut by hand."

The ribs were then clad by a boatbuilding technique, involving strips of lathe and cloth, and finally concrete or plaster. "So we end up with these very complex forms that are kind of a perfect combination of this rapid prototyping technology, and very traditional craftsmen coming in and doing the final finishes," says McDowell.

PAGES 92–93: The isolated House of El sits atop a natural promontory in this conceptual piece.

THESE PAGES: A swarm of Kryptonian security craft position themselves around the House of El's hangar to cut off escape by air.

FLORA AND FAUNA

The city of Kandor is evidence that the Kryptonians have demanded too much of their world, but their planet still houses many vibrant specimens of alien evolution. Deep in the wilds live creatures still untouched by genetic tampering, and the king of these is the Rondor Beast. Taller than an apartment complex, it shambles through the tree line and frightens flocks of avians with each ground-shaking step.

The art department looked at Krypton's biosphere through the eyes of zoologists and produced charts indicating the relative sizes of plants and animals on scales that indicate that some things are beyond the control of the Kryptonian Council. Intriguing plant names mentioned in one draft of the screenplay include Blood Morels and Morningstar Seeds.

The most endearing Kryptonian animal in *Man of Steel* is H'raka, Jor-El's faithful "war kite" who exhibits a dog's unshakeable loyalty to its master. Zack Snyder imagined that H'raka and its fellow flyers had been selectively bred by the Kryptonians for optimal speed and beauty, with thoroughbred stables just off-screen and a pureblood pedigree for H'raka that may have stretched back for centuries. H'raka's wings were inspired by the shape of the maple seeds that pinwheel to earth in autumn, while its head is derived from a leopard seal.

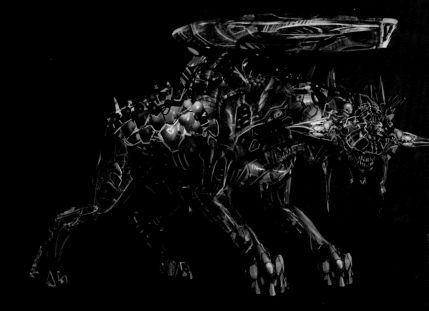

PAGES 96–97: A Rondor beast bellows and a flock of avians takes flight, in this piece that depicts a scene within Krypton's wilderness.

ABOVE: This cyborg war dog was developed during preproduction but did not make it into the final version of the film.

BELOW AND LEFT: Flowing curves and waving tendrils are common elements among the specimens of Krypton's native flora and fauna.

OPPOSITE: A digital model (top) and finished VFX frame (bottom) showing the endlessly loyal war kite, H'raka.

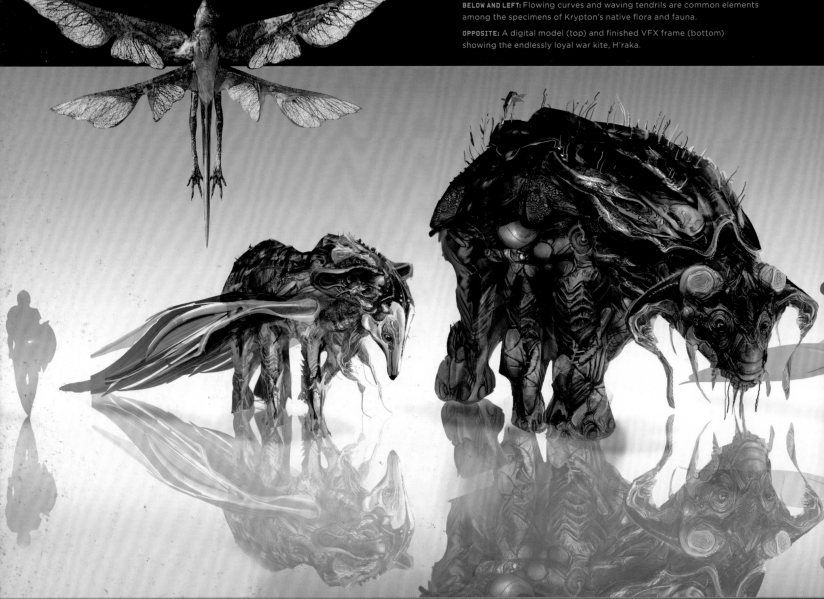

"It's like a seal-slash-dragonfly," says Snyder. "We wanted a sympathetic face, which is why we picked the seal. And they're slightly old-school, since Jor-El is more subtly connected with nature. Unlike Zod, who flies one of the attack ships."

Design sketches for H'raka outlined the process by which the robot Kelex could plug into the front end of the saddle, becoming an in-flight monitor to provide navigation and communication data. During filming, Russell Crowe performed his H'raka scenes while sitting on a gimbal-mounted foam armature in front of a green screen. Green-shrouded puppeteers helped maneuver this "mechanical bull" into a convincing illusion of life.

If untamed evolution produced the Rondor Beast, and careful breeding produced H'raka, what would happen if the Kryptonians went all out with their genetic tailoring? The art department came up with the horrifying answer, through pieces depicting biomechanical attack beasts. The cyborg war dog is a spike-headed hound studded with spines and weighted down by a heavy plasma cannon fused to its shoulderblades. Although this particular creature did not make it into the finished film, concept art hints at how it might have appeared.

THESE PAGES: An aerial view of the Genesis Chamber shows off the scale of the planet's cloning operation, emphasizing the peril of Jor-El's mad mission.

ABOVE: The Genesis Chamber as it appears in the finished film.

THE GENESIS CHAMBER

There hasn't been anything natural about the Kryptonians for centuries, and Jor-El and Lara's decision to proceed with an organic birth is an act of heresy. The Council's justification for their society's genetic programming, and its associated caste system, is the Genesis Chamber.

As its name implies, the Genesis Chamber is the source of all life on Krypton, the crèche from which new citizens are produced according to society's needs. After the planet's destruction, a smaller laboratory containing the same technology becomes the only solution for staving off the extinction of the Kryptonian race.

"The Kryptonians are all born out of the Genesis Chamber," explains Zack Snyder. "Their brains and physiologies are altered to the purpose that they're meant to perform. If yours is 'Warrior,' your methods are going to be more brutal. It's not your fault; it's just the way you were made."

Alex McDowell's team needed to design the Genesis Chamber by deducing its mechanisms, which rely on the same dwindling power source that ultimately dooms the Kryptonian people. "The energy of the core of the planet is pumped up through these stone veins or vessels, pulling liquid that is pure energy up and feeding the growth of the population," says McDowell. "[This is] the womb of the planet. The babies are all being brought up in the planet's amniotic fluid. And that becomes a symbol in the scout ship that carries its own Genesis Chamber and represents the last hope of propagating the future of Krypton."

Inspiration for the Genesis Chamber's strings of embryonic spheres came from morning dew on grass blades, sticky balls of mucilage on carnivorous sundew plants, and translucent clusters of frog eggs. Layered, calcified meshes cover the central tank, their patterns derived from fractal algorithms. The structure enclosing the chamber looks as if it is composed of volcanic plumes that have solidified into a tabletop of flat-capped circles.

As the planet's birthing hub, the Genesis Chamber is defended by its own robotic legion. Art for the chamber's "aquabots" showed off multiple designs, one of them possessing the extendable tail of a stingray. Another aquabot could shift into attack stance by splaying its six articulated limbs, like an angry hermit crab flipped onto its back.

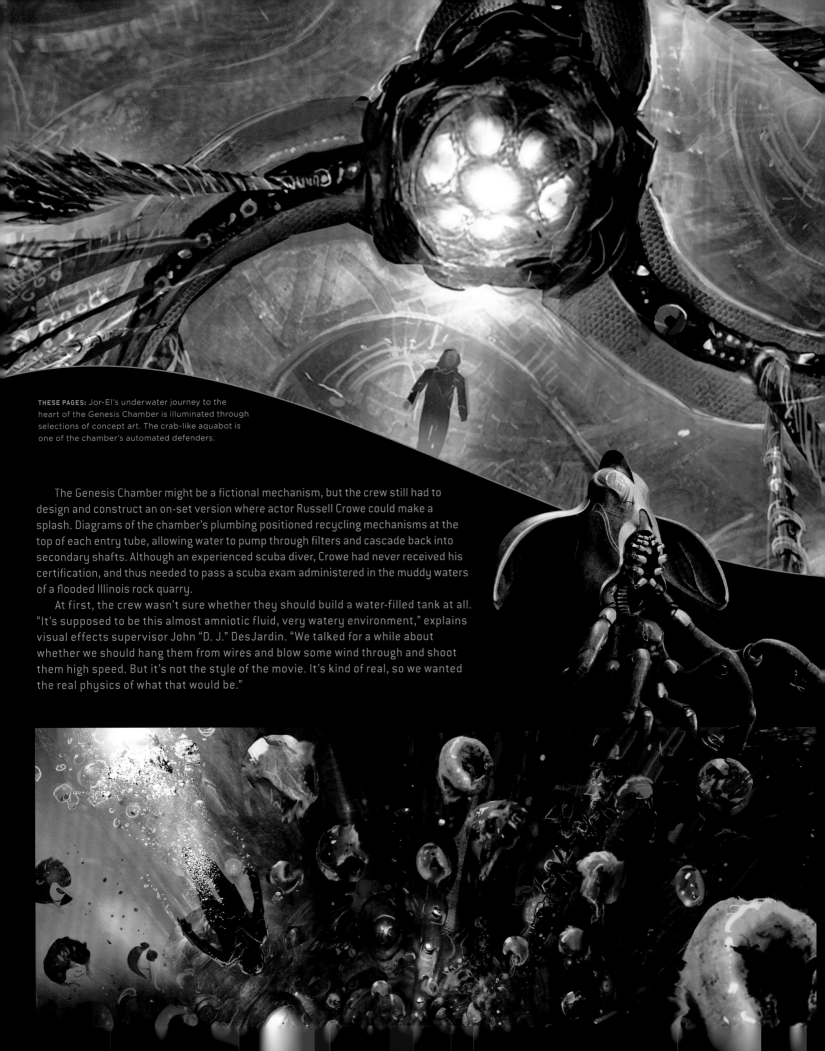

THESE PAGES: Jor-El's underwater journey to the heart of the Genesis Chamber is illuminated through selections of concept art. The crab-like aquabot is one of the chamber's automated defenders.

The Genesis Chamber might be a fictional mechanism, but the crew still had to design and construct an on-set version where actor Russell Crowe could make a splash. Diagrams of the chamber's plumbing positioned recycling mechanisms at the top of each entry tube, allowing water to pump through filters and cascade back into secondary shafts. Although an experienced scuba diver, Crowe had never received his certification, and thus needed to pass a scuba exam administered in the muddy waters of a flooded Illinois rock quarry.

At first, the crew wasn't sure whether they should build a water-filled tank at all. "It's supposed to be this almost amniotic fluid, very watery environment," explains visual effects supervisor John "D. J." DesJardin. "We talked for a while about whether we should hang them from wires and blow some wind through and shoot them high speed. But it's not the style of the movie. It's kind of real, so we wanted the real physics of what that would be."

Charles Roven explains that the Genesis Chamber is one of the Kryptonian locations that received the biggest assist from post-production visual effects: "The reality is that with the Genesis Chamber, we simply created it through visual effects. We created landmarks for Russell to swim through, and then we created the effects around those landmarks. So he was swimming in a tank inside a lit soundstage, but he was swimming with the intention of this being where the embryos are being guarded by the robotic androids. He had his costume on, but everything else was a visual effect."

LAST HOPE

"There hasn't been a natural childbirth on Krypton in thousands of years," says David Goyer. "We decided that Kal's should be the first natural childbirth on Krypton in years and years. So it's a very special event. But because Jor-El and Lara decide to have a natural childbirth on Krypton, that in and of itself is a crime potentially punishable by death."

This is a risk the couple is willing to take, even without the ticking clock imposed by the looming destruction of their planet. Jor-El and Lara seek to create a child free from genetic predetermination and the laws governing the castes. In short, they want to create the first Kryptonian in memory who is truly free.

Kal-El takes only a few breaths of the air of his birthworld before he is secured inside the craft that will speed him away from condemned Krypton. The rocket is a pleasing interplay of grooves and planes, with bulbous protrusions that don't take anything away from its overall sense of streamlining. Deep, parallel notches that could be engine vents or air intakes hint that the craft is a lot faster than it looks, and indeed much of its interior is given over to the machinery that powers the Phantom Drive. One end of the rocket is capped by a hemispherical heat shield, proudly adorned with the insignia of the House of El—the Kryptonian symbol for hope.

Jor-El tucks something into the pod along with his son, revealed as the House of El command key that he has unplugged from the Genesis Chamber. This tool is a one-piece wedge carved from polished stone or a similar substance. Its teeth are of varying lengths and thicknesses and are dotted with circular holes as if bubbles had formed inside its structure through volcanism.

THESE PAGES: His time running out, Jor-El prepares the craft that will bring his son to a safer place.

PAGES 106–107: With the angry orb of Rao at their backs, a Kryptonian armada encroaches on the remote stretch of land occupied by the House of El.

Ultimately, Jor-El makes a stand to defend his legacy and his vision for Krypton. He first visits the House of El's armory chamber, where a pod can lower from the ceiling and close its petals around a visitor. It encases the wearer in head-to-toe battle armor before it retracts.

Sadly, Jor-El cannot succeed in his quixotic quest, and everything he fights for will soon face ruin. The destruction of Krypton is a fundamental piece of the Superman legend—it's literally the first panel of 1938's *Action Comics* #1. "Zack and Alex and I talked about that explosion," says DesJardin. "Matter gets thrown out, but most of it's right there. The planet is just a rubble field being held together by the gravity of its core, which has been ignited almost like a failed star."

ABOVE: This petal-shaped structure encloses Jor-El and outfits him in armor.

RIGHT: Jor-El and his loyal war kite H'raka await their fates.

PAGES 110–111: Within the cavernous space of the Black Zero, Zod's insurgents interact with hemispherical display screens.

BLACK ZERO

General Zod and his revolutionaries underestimate the inertia that keeps the Council atop Krypton's power structure. Their sentence for attempting a coup d'état? Three hundred cycles of somatic reconditioning in the Phantom Zone. In *Man of Steel*, this punishment is carried out with the help of a prison barge labeled the Black Zero.

"We imagined that the Black Zero was a quite different kind of craft," says Alex McDowell. "If the Kryptonians put away their ships—and that's the idea, that they gave up space travel—the Black Zero is something they basically pulled out of mothballs to use for this sentencing. They've actually had to kind of hot-wire it and recycle the technology to make it work again. The Black Zero is highly chaotic."

Zod and the others are placed within cryostasis chambers in the Black Zero's hibernation bay. The ship's interior is textured with crawling cables and dangling tubes, where everything is disorganized and distressed. The surroundings have a biological aesthetic that seems more sinister than the largely noble environments of Krypton.

"It takes so much power to use the Phantom Zone generator to transport that there's only a tiny amount of real estate that's available to the Kryptonians themselves," explains McDowell. "So you're actually inside the engine at all times. It's an organic space, asymmetric."

The Black Zero isn't representative of every vessel in the Kryptonian navy, and creating each unique craft is an intensive process. "We extrapolated from this exterior what the interior might look like, starting with engines as giant spheres," says McDowell. "Those are the energy sources that reoccur on a lot of the ships." One piece of concept art laid out the entire lineup of the planet's armada aligned for comparative scale. Hammerheads are large battle cruisers, Scarabs smaller fighters. Both belong to the loyalist Sapphire Guard and are seen only fleetingly in the film.

OPPOSITE BOTTOM LEFT: A Kryptonian escape pod evokes thoughts of life preservation with its heart-like shape.

ABOVE: The interior of the Black Zero is a riot of tubing and tendrils. Its escape pods are polished to an ebony sheen.

PAGES 114–115: In both color and contour, the Kryptonian drop ships are a sharp contrast to the backdrop of a threatened Metropolis.

The Phantom Zone projector sits in orbit above Krypton. Three satellites in triangular formation emit an unfamiliar energy, projecting a distortion field between the vertices that glistens with the shifting colors of a soap bubble. This shunts the Black Zero into subspace, where it remains until Krypton's explosion rattles its extradimensional cage.

After he is freed, General Zod makes the Black Zero his flagship. The craft sports a profile that's unique among sci-fi vessels, with a vertical configuration resembling a mobile skyscraper. In fact, one of the first pieces of concept art depicted how the Black Zero might look above the urban canyons of a modern Earth city.

"The fun thing was to try and make a ship that was very different from the way we understand spaceships to be," says McDowell. "So we put it in the context of our Metropolis skyline to see what this enormous vertical object would look like as an alien ship."

Like a pirate ship deploying its longboats, the Black Zero can release a squadron of drop ships for shuttling passengers to land. Each drop ship is the size of a helicopter troop carrier and wears a beetle's glossy carapace, possessing a profile that resembles a severed vertebra. "The drop ships came from kind of a horsefly," explains McDowell. "Just a nasty little heavy-duty bug that clearly states its bad intent from its silhouette. . . . As a ship, it can spin in midair and be firing on all guns at the same time."

In one design concept, the drop ships huddled together on the Black Zero's hull for storage and transport. "We imagined this random clustering of thirty or forty of these on the exterior," says McDowell. "So when the Black Zero sends off the forces, they drop off the face of it and it really looks kind of nasty."

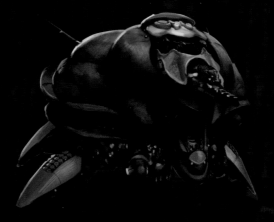

OPPOSITE MIDDLE AND LEFT: Each compact, weapons-studded drop ship is small but packs a big punch.

OPPOSITE BOTTOM LEFT: The World Engine belches fire and smoke as it wreaks havoc.

TOP: The crackling energy extended from each orbital vertex creates a portal that leads to the Phantom Zone.

RIGHT: Zod's soldiers, having investigated another dead colony, return to the Black Zero.

PAGES 120–121: Zod's soldiers come upon a long-dead Kryptonian colonist, another reminder of the extinction of their species.

THE DEAD COLONIES

Earth isn't the Black Zero's first stop. General Zod takes his warship on a tour of forgotten Kryptonian settlements across the galaxy, all of them abandoned generations ago when Krypton scrapped its space program. Zod hopes that survivors might still be found who can join his cause and swell his ranks.

"When they get released from the Phantom Zone after Krypton's destruction, they retrofit the Phantom Drive projector into a hyperdrive so they can warp space," explains Zack Snyder. "They go to all the Kryptonian colonies, where the people have been unsupplied and in these hostile environments. And they died off."

Concept art depicts Zod's insurgents in full-body spacesuits fanning out across the surfaces of lifeless alien planets. These environments were built as practical sets and dressed with skeletons in Kryptonian armor. Half buried in the sand, and wearing the grins of skinless skulls, these lost Kryptonians seem like fallen crusaders who never received the honor of burial back in their home kingdoms.

"[It's] a small bit of backstory, but it tells how they weaponize themselves and how they gave themselves the ability to attack Earth," says Alex McDowell, walking through the process by which Zod acquired his impressive arsenal. Krypton's age of expansion lasted one hundred thousand years, but now no traces of it remain other than rusted weapons and the World Engine—the terraforming marvel left over from the bygone Kryptonian space program.

"You can't show every little detail and nuance of what's been created by the art department or the props guys on screen," says DesJardin, "but the fact that it's been thought about does come out. It comes in the design of the spaceships; it comes out in the design of the outposts we go to. It's all about the roots."

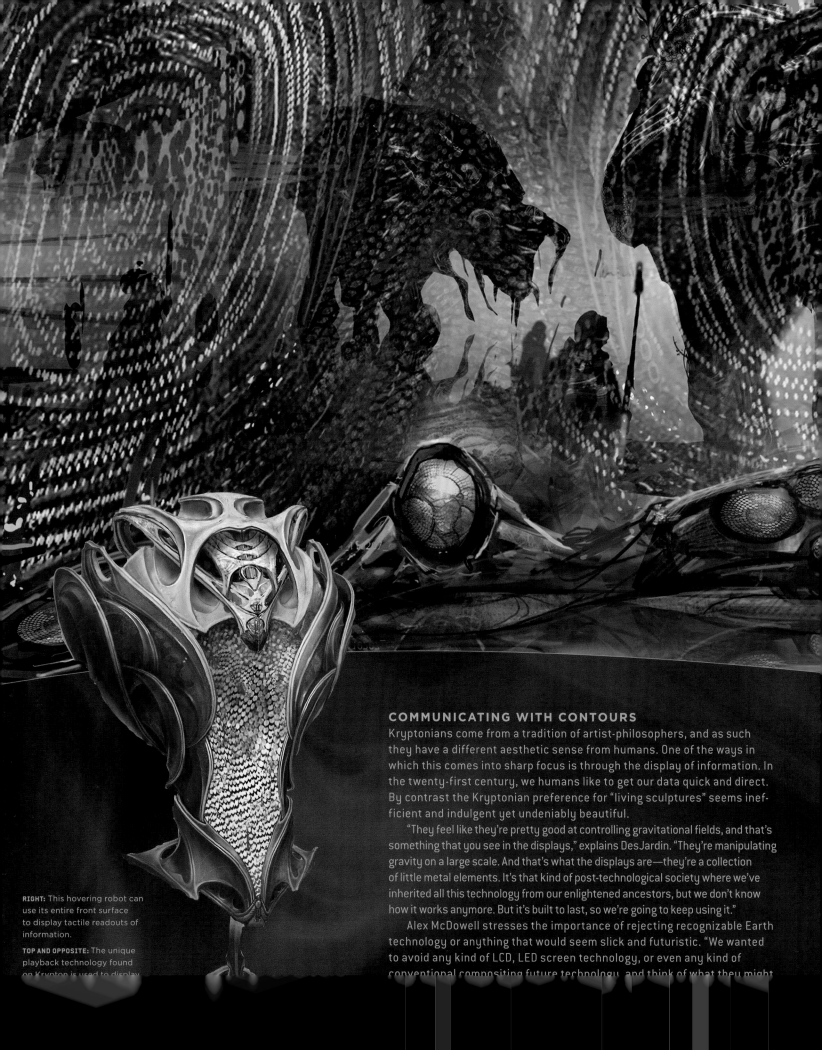

COMMUNICATING WITH CONTOURS

Kryptonians come from a tradition of artist-philosophers, and as such they have a different aesthetic sense from humans. One of the ways in which this comes into sharp focus is through the display of information. In the twenty-first century, we humans like to get our data quick and direct. By contrast the Kryptonian preference for "living sculptures" seems inefficient and indulgent yet undeniably beautiful.

"They feel like they're pretty good at controlling gravitational fields, and that's something that you see in the displays," explains DesJardin. "They're manipulating gravity on a large scale. And that's what the displays are—they're a collection of little metal elements. It's that kind of post-technological society where we've inherited all this technology from our enlightened ancestors, but we don't know how it works anymore. But it's built to last, so we're going to keep using it."

Alex McDowell stresses the importance of rejecting recognizable Earth technology or anything that would seem slick and futuristic. "We wanted to avoid any kind of LCD, LED screen technology, or even any kind of conventional compositing future technology, and think of what they might

RIGHT: This hovering robot can use its entire front surface to display tactile readouts of information.

TOP AND OPPOSITE: The unique playback technology found on Krypton is used to display

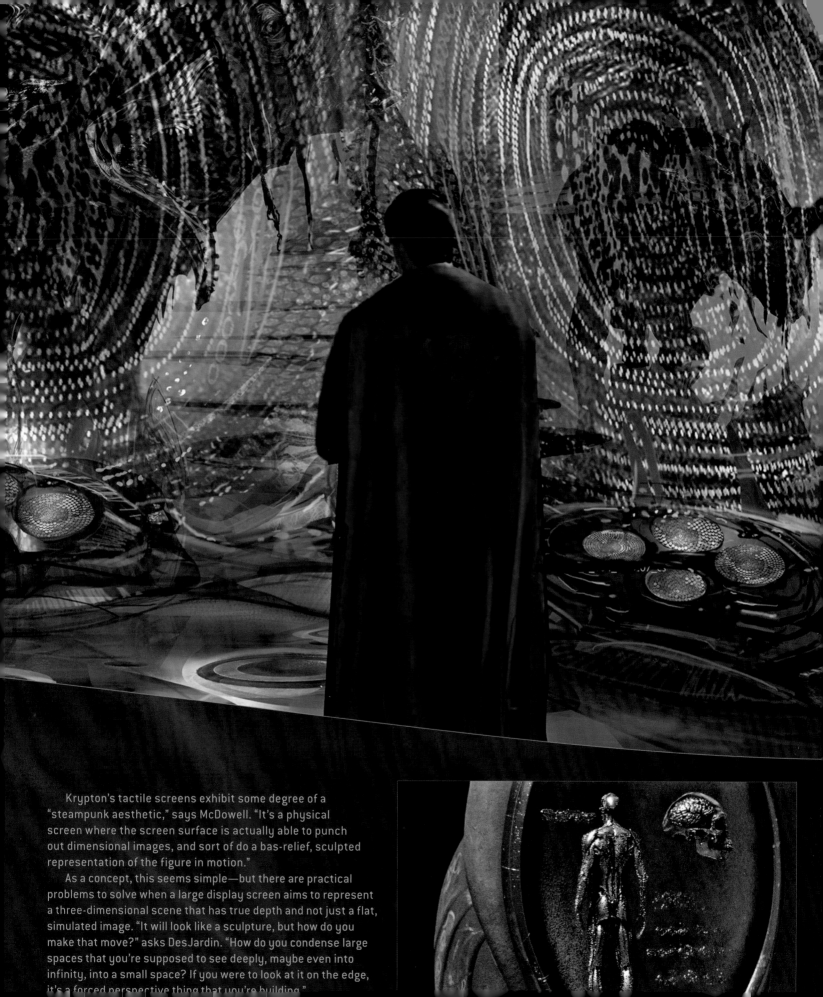

Krypton's tactile screens exhibit some degree of a "steampunk aesthetic," says McDowell. "It's a physical screen where the screen surface is actually able to punch out dimensional images, and sort of do a bas-relief, sculpted representation of the figure in motion."

As a concept, this seems simple—but there are practical problems to solve when a large display screen aims to represent a three-dimensional scene that has true depth and not just a flat, simulated image. "It will look like a sculpture, but how do you make that move?" asks DesJardin. "How do you condense large spaces that you're supposed to see deeply, maybe even into infinity, into a small space? If you were to look at it on the edge, it's a forced perspective thing that you're building."

THE SCOUT SHIP

The final piece of Kryptonian design is ironically found on Earth. Just as Kal-El's rocket arrived in Kansas, a scout ship left Krypton during the planet's age of exploration and long ago crashed in the glacier fields above the Arctic Circle.

The scout ship is benevolently organic. Its shape is that of a garden slug, with the nubs on its ventral surface resembling the legs of a newborn caterpillar. Its paleness is the chromatic opposite of the drop ships' hostile sheen, with the shadowing of natural light used to call attention to the specifics of its form. The *Man of Steel* design team used photo reference of an antique, baroque-detailed desk to find inspiration for its surface. From a distance, the scout ship's monochromatic hull could be mistaken for the elongated skull of a horse.

McDowell underscores the intentional contrast between the Black Zero—"very messy in all its aspects"—and the scout ship: "[It] is really pretty clean and relatively bright and well-ordered."

Inside the scout ship, Kryptonian artifacts lie in wait, including environmental skinsuits. One of these becomes Superman's costume. At a key moment in the film, the scout ship powers up after eighteen thousand years of inactivity. Rising into the air, it sloughs off its shroud of ice and later nestles into the windswept crest of a mountaintop. It stands as a metaphor that melding Krypton with Earth is not only possible, but pleasing.

PAGES 124–125: Locked away beneath arctic ice for millennia, the Kryptonian scout ship becomes Clark Kent's most tangible link to a vanished heritage.

OPPOSITE TOP: A 3-D exterior model of the scout ship showcases its knobby, shell-like hull.

LEFT AND ABOVE: The gentle lines of the scout ship's interior and exterior speak to its harmony with nature.

WELCOME TO EARTH

ONCE YOU ACCEPT THE PREMISE behind the Superman story, you've bought into a science-fiction universe and the existence of physics-defying superpowers. Because this conceptual leap comes with the territory, Zack Snyder sought to maximize audience immersion by normalizing every supporting element. In *Man of Steel*, Earth's environments ground viewers with sights that could be taking place right outside their windows.

"Zack is known as a very stylized shooter and a master of surreal worlds and visual effects," says co-producer Wes Coller. "And although we use visual effects to help tell the story, on Earth we wanted it to feel real. When it came to the scenes that took place here, I think we were less tasked with world-building than we were with story building."

Man of Steel takes place in every corner of our globe, from Kansas cornfields to an atoll in the Indian Ocean. Each stage helps chart Clark's journey from victim to outsider, until he finally accepts the mantle of a hero.

"It creates a language that feels slightly more immersive than something that's to be stepped back from and admired," says Coller. "It brings you into that world."

THESE PAGES: A Kryptonian drop ship sweeps in for a strafing pass on downtown Smallville in this conceptual piece.

PAGES 128-129: The barn at the Kent farmhouse holds the key to Kal-El's past.

NORTHERN JOURNEYS

When Clark Kent first appears in *Man of Steel*, he's far from the cornfields of Kansas or the newsroom of the *Daily Planet*. Viewers catch up to Clark during his quest to find his place in this world. As a spiritual tug drives him north, Clark earns meal money by fishing for crabs and busing tables.

"I feel like it was much more realistic to see him have these odd jobs," says Debbie Snyder. "In today's economic times, his kind of trajectory is much more relatable to the average American. Even though we'll never know what it's like to fly, if we can find a way to relate to him, we'll care more about him as a character. And at some point in everyone's life they're struggling to find out what they believe in, what their purpose in life is. We've all been at this crossroads and sometimes we feel a little lost."

Clark knows he's not like other people, but he hasn't yet learned that he's an alien exile from the planet Krypton. And, even though his adoptive father Jonathan Kent urged him to keep his powers under wraps, Clark can't ignore danger and injustice when he has the ability to set things right. "It's in his nature to help people," says Debbie Snyder. "But when people get too close and start to get suspicious, he has to move on."

During his time on the fringe of life, Clark signs on as a greenhorn crewman aboard the crab boat *Debbie Sue* to ply the Bering Sea. Filming for the sequence took place in the choppy waters near Vancouver Island.

"We actually brought that crab boat up from Seattle," says producer Charles Roven. "It wasn't that there weren't any crab boats in Vancouver; it was that Zack wanted a particular crab boat. One that had a certain kind of deck and a captain's wheelhouse."

Henry Cavill got a crash course in the life of a crabber before setting out on the water and had to fight back seasickness as he rode out thirty-foot swells. "I'm sure they probably looked at us like we had two heads at first," he says, of the *Debbie Sue*'s crew. "The things that film crews need, it's just so alien on a crab boat."

Vancouver Island also served as the backdrop for the oil rig explosion that forces Clark to abandon the *Debbie Sue* and do what he can to help those in danger. The oil rig's landing platform wasn't shot on stage, but out-of-doors in Vancouver, with strategic green screen backdrops inserted for later scenery fill-ins. "We built a whole platform for the helicopter to land on," says Charles Roven. "It was an amazing piece of engineering."

On the island's shoreline, the crew filmed the shirtless Clark's emergence from near-freezing waters. "It was quite tough just to keep a positive mental attitude when we were standing outside on a green screen for the oil rig stuff," says Cavill. "And we had the big Black Hawk coast guard helicopter come in. And when you're in sixty-, seventy-mile-per-hour winds, in the rotor wash with your shirt off, and it's winter in Vancouver—I mean, I'm not one to complain, but goodness me."

The inner workings of the rig, including its pipe-and-valve architecture and the gouts of fire that menace Clark, provided another challenge for Roven's team. "We built that, too," he says. "And that was all shot practically."

THESE PAGES: The fiery ruin visited on this offshore oil rig presents the kind of challenge that can only be tackled by someone with Clark's unique abilities.

ABOVE: In this still from *Man of Steel*, Clark Kent tests the limits of what he can endure.

Clark is forced to ditch the *Debbie Sue* after the oil rig incident, and viewers pick up with him in Canada's Northwest Territories, working at the Bearcat Bar outside Yellowknife. Humiliated at having to back down from a bully, he lashes out in the parking lot by jackknifing the troublemaker's eighteen-wheeler. "It was a complete practical effect," says Roven of the folded semi, shot on location in Vancouver using no post-production trickery. "We did that to a truck and its rig."

An inner voice draws Clark to Ellesmere Island, a Canadian possession north of the Arctic Circle near Greenland. He finds himself in the company of *Daily Planet* reporter Lois Lane, who steps out of her helicopter to see that the United States Northern Command—

U.S. Northcom—has set up shop to investigate the mystery of a buried artifact. Northcom has brought in a thermal meltdown generator to bore a hole through the ice, but it is Clark whose destiny is linked to the discovery. The Ellesmere incident provides the inhabitants of Earth with their first real evidence of the existence of ancient aliens.

A desolate glacier north of Whistler, British Columbia, stood in for Ellesmere Island. "There's something about a real glacier that is pretty hard to replicate," says Wes Coller. The production crew needed to construct a military operations base on the empty spot, a task made more complicated due to the site's remoteness. "We flew helicopters up there and built it in one day," says Charles Roven, "and then flew helicopters up there with our actors and shot it in one day."

THESE PAGES: Pushed too far, Clark evens the score with a bully with a spectacular show of damage to his eighteen-wheeler.

PAGES 136–137: This piece captures the tranquility of Smallville at midday, before Zod's Kryptonians turn the town into a war zone.

SMALLVILLE

Unlike previous Superman origin stories, Clark Kent's history as a child growing up in Smallville is told entirely in flashback. Kevin Costner and Diane Lane, as Clark's adoptive parents Jonathan and Martha Kent, provide the love and moral guidance that give the future Man of Steel an empathy that is anything but alien.

Writer David Goyer wanted Jonathan and Martha to be younger and more relatable than the characters in the comics, who sometimes seemed more like grandparents than parents, and the warm toughness of Costner and Lane seemed an ideal match. Goyer also wanted to explore the kind of people who would raise an extraterrestrial baby as their own without knowing what he might be capable of. "We deal a lot with the anxiety that the Kents have as adoptive parents," he says. "They don't know if his real parents are still out there or not, or if they'll show up one day. Even when [Clark] was very little, even without seeing him perform any kind of superhuman feat, the other kids sense that he's different. And because of that they persecute him."

This is a worry for the Kents, but it's a more immediate problem for young Clark. He takes abuse from classmates including Pete Ross, Ken Braverman, and Whitney Fordman—all of them callbacks to characters from previous eras of Superman's history.

"I think there were a lot of kids that bullied him," says Debbie Snyder. "It's harder to stand up against the bullies for fear of being bullied yourself. I don't think he was alone; there were just a lot of people who didn't understand him. And [who] were probably a little afraid of him."

Young Clark Kent is played at different life stages by Cooper Timberline (Clark at age nine) and Dylan Sprayberry (Clark at age thirteen). Costume designer Michael Wilkinson outfitted each Clark in clothes appropriate to the timeline and to suggest a boy who was always in hiding. "He doesn't wear anything that brings a lot of attention to himself," he says. "He wears old hoodies and T-shirts. He just wants to blend in with the other guys."

The Smallville, Kansas, flashbacks were the very first scenes captured for *Man of Steel*, with the sequence of a school bus crashing through a bridge railing the top item on the crew's schedule. Several American towns had landed on the short list for becoming the latest big-screen Smallville, but Plano, Illinois, emerged as the clear winner.

"I counted up about fifty-six cities and small towns outside of Chicago," says supervising location manager Bill Doyle, who hoped to cover his filming needs for big-city Metropolis and rural Smallville within a small patch of U.S. geography. "We ended up with three good ones, and I sat with the mayors of each, [but] this was the one that had everything that Alex and Zack liked."

TOP RIGHT: Dylan Sprayberry as the teenage Clark conveys the pain of growing up with powers that no one can understand.

MIDDLE RIGHT: Cooper Timberline plays Clark Kent at the tender age of nine.

BOTTOM RIGHT: Martha Kent is a constant presence throughout Clark's growth, reassuring him that he will always be loved despite his differences.

OPPOSITE: Dylan Sprayberry as the older Clark learns the secret of the space capsule that carried him to Earth.

PAGES 140–141: Superman faces a deadly, Western-style showdown on the streets of Smallville.

The Kent farmhouse represents the upbringing that shaped Clark Kent's conscience, and it is a cornerstone of the Superman legend. It was critical that the team get it right, but the logistics got complicated after each of the two perfect sites near Plano could only meet half of the crew's needs. "We found the perfect farmhouse on the wrong property, and no farmhouse on the property that we wanted," explains Charles Roven. "So we ended up building our own house from scratch in the style of the farmhouse we liked on the property that we wanted."

That didn't solve all the problems. The land surrounding the relocated farmhouse had an ideal photographic horizon made of rolling fields, but the property owners had their eye on crops that wouldn't have looked sufficiently cinematic. "We wanted cornfields, but they decided that they were growing soybeans," says Roven. "So we had to come in there four months earlier and lease out everything that you can see around the farmhouse to make sure that we could put corn there." The production crew received regular reports to learn how fast their corn was growing and to make sure they kept on track for the shoot.

Downtown Smallville is the location of one of the film's biggest action set pieces. When the city gets caught in the middle of a fight between the U.S. military and Zod's superpowered Kryptonians, its infrastructure takes a major hit. "[Plano] had had a train wreck that took out three blocks of their main street, on one side of it," says Charles Roven. And as tragic as the accident had been, the damage done to the surrounding area proved ideal for the type of action *Man of Steel* needed to stage. "It couldn't have been more perfect for us, because we wanted to build Smallville, and then we wanted to destroy it."

Those empty sites in Plano's shopping district allowed the crew to erect false storefronts in their locations, then choreograph the action around them. Before arriving in Plano, Bill Doyle's crew used a combination of location photos and computer modeling to produce a 3-D model of the downtown district. "Zack can scout that in previz," he says, referring to the technique of previsualization, or outlining complex scenes prior to the start of filming. "So by the time he gets to the town it's familiar to him."

Adds Alex McDowell, "We could really turn it into a backlot and build our own town and blow it up. So the Sears was built between the bank and one of the buildings and plugged the hole there. It enabled us to crash the locomotive into that and blow it up."

Charles Roven points out that this Smallville is contemporary and familiar, in another example of *Man of Steel*'s focus on realism. "We purposefully

added iconic elements to make them that much more typically American," he says. "We wanted a Sears. We wanted a 7-Eleven. We wanted to use these elements in the small town of Smallville because we found that to be typically American."

Debbie Snyder saw an opportunity for realism of another sort, by not treating Smallville as if it were an over-idealized, Norman Rockwell postcard. "We wanted it to be reflective of what's happening in small towns today," she says, "where there are certain stores that have closed down because they couldn't make ends meet."

Smallville is a setting that values authenticity over perfection and it's clear that the town is an honest slice of everyday America. It's also clear that Kal-El got pretty lucky when his crash-landing provided him with such humble yet honorable beginnings.

ABOVE: Zod and his insurgents make a terrifying arrival at the Kent farmhouse.

OPPOSITE TOP: The Kent farmhouse is Clark's childhood home, and to see it damaged weighs heavy on his heart.

OPPOSITE BOTTOM: Treatments of the Kent farmhouse show how its exterior weathers over the decades.

U.S. NORTHCOM

The U.S. military is the first to recognize the presence of something alien on Earth. Their dig on Ellesmere Island brings Lois Lane into their orbit and starts the chain of events that leads to Clark claiming his destiny as Superman.

In *Man of Steel*, General Swanwick of U.S. Northern Command initially plays the part of antagonist as he carries out his mission to "deter, prevent, and defeat threats and aggression aimed at the United States." Swanwick thinks Superman is one of those threats, but once he perceives the true danger from Zod's insurgents he doesn't hesitate to match the planet's most advanced fighting force against a legion of superpowered Kryptonians.

The importance of U.S. Northcom to the story inspired the *Man of Steel* crew to secure the formal cooperation of the U.S. Department of Defense. "They don't demand script approval," says producer Charles Roven, "but they demand approval of what the military does. And that was okay, because we wanted it to be real."

Debbie Snyder knew this partnership would be important, not only for the film's verisimilitude, but also to ensure that *Man of Steel* portrayed the armed forces in the proper light. "It was really important to Zack, who has a lot of friends who are in the military, that we were as authentic as possible," she says. "Not only do we have all the hardware, but we also have their expertise, so we could ask them questions about what would happen in an instance like this. David Goyer worked with them on the dialogue for the pilots. You get an authenticity that you wouldn't have otherwise."

Adds Charles Roven, "Zack wanted to give the film this feeling that, even though we're dealing with a Super Hero, it could actually happen. And having the Department of Defense and the military there to make sure that the things that we were doing were credible only added to that sense of realism."

The command center of the U.S. Northcom was shot in Vancouver, in an abandoned youth detention center that the crew took over and modified for their use. Exteriors—including the prisoner handoff between Northcom forces and Subcommander Faora—were shot on the dry lake beds of Mojave, California, at Edwards Air Force Base.

PAGES 144–145: The familiar meets the unthinkable in preproduction art for the Battle of Smallville.

THESE PAGES: A stricken A-10 Warthog veers dangerously close to the pavement while downtown Smallville burns in the background.

ABOVE: Henry Cavill's Superman, backed by military personnel, stands on the barren salt flats surrounding Edwards Air Force Base.

OPPOSITE: This frame from *Man of Steel* shows the bustling Ellesmere Island station manned by U.S. Northcom.

PAGES 150–151: Preproduction art for the Ellesmere Island station depicts a hive of secretive military activity.

"The whole base was jazzed," remembers Roven. "And we were jazzed about the base, because Edwards is a legendary place. They were all Superman fans. And if you can't be in the movie business, you probably want to be a test pilot."

The Department of Defense joined forces with the administrators of Plano, Illinois, and the *Man of Steel* filming crew to stage the Battle of Smallville. In what is essentially the first strike of an alien invasion, an American town is leveled by raw, incalculable power.

"We had a lot of pyrotechnics and helicopters and military and stunts," says Debbie Snyder, "and the town was great because we closed off a good portion of their main street. We were able to completely close it down. We had the help of

In the film, the skies above Smallville swarm with military hardware including the MH-6 Little Bird light helicopter and the A-10 Warthog ground-attack aircraft. The A-10, which was built to take out armored vehicles with its nose-mounted Gatling gun, is put to the test when it's matched against bulletproof Kryptonian skin. Many of these aircraft soon wind up in the streets of Smallville, torn to pieces.

"The plane crashes are going to be CG, but the aftermath used real parts from planes that we got from the military," says Debbie Snyder. "We got to go through their airplane graveyard and pick out a bunch of parts that we dressed the city in."

In one piece of concept art, a confident Faora strides toward a downed soldier, like a predator cornering wounded prey. Ready to go down shooting, the human pulls his sidearm and takes careful aim at his executioner. This wordless image summed up the character of Colonel Hardy, a Northcom officer with guts to spare.

"She throws a van at my helicopter and knocks it out of the sky," says Christopher Meloni, who plays Hardy. "I immediately say to myself, 'I want to meet that woman.' But she's a little aggressive, so I have to pull out my machine gun and pop some caps. That doesn't stop her, though."

Debbie Snyder admits that Faora seems to have marked Hardy for special attention. "She has it in for him," she says. "There's this tension between the two of them that I think is pretty magical on the screen. Zod and Faora don't have a sense of morality, but our soldiers on Earth do. And as much as they have this similarity that they're both warriors, they come at it from two different perspectives."

METROPOLIS

Metropolis is Superman's home base in the comics—a fictional stand-in for New York City that's sometimes dressed up in art deco or retro-futurism. For *Man of Steel*, the crew didn't want Metropolis to feel the least bit sci-fi. This led them to Chicago, but it also meant avoiding using the actual Windy City as a backdrop.

"It's not Chicago," says Debbie Snyder. "We changed the skyline; there's no recognizable buildings. It's Metropolis. [But] we shot it in Chicago, so it should feel like a modern city and just as real as anything else."

Christopher Nolan helped lead the crew to Chicago, having used it as the real-world version of Gotham City in *Batman Begins* and *The Dark Knight*. "I told Zack that Chicago is a great place to film, but I left it up to him as to whether it fit his image of what he wanted Metropolis to be," he says. "But Chicago

was so welcoming to us on the *Dark Knight* films and we had such great experiences there while making it. And from a visual point of view, Chicago presents all manner of different architectural sources and approaches."

Reference maps for *Man of Steel*'s Metropolis setting hewed closely to the geography developed in the comics: New Troy is an analogue for Manhattan Island, and Metropolis's outer boroughs include the Bakerline and Queensland Park. During production, the crew determined that their version of Metropolis sat on the Eastern Seaboard near Norfolk, Virginia.

The *Man of Steel* crew moved into Chicago on September 1, 2011, shooting on location for two weeks. Some interior sets and action sequences were later shot on set in Vancouver.

Metropolis wouldn't feel like home without the *Daily Planet*. Not only is the newspaper office the place where Clark Kent draws his paycheck, through its journalistic integrity it also mirrors Superman's battle against corrupt forces. For *Man of Steel*, the exterior of the glass-and-steel Illinois Center at 111 East Wacker became the *Daily Planet* headquarters. Constructed in 1967, the building is an example of the supreme practicality in urban postwar architecture, and its blocky design couldn't be more different than the graceful contours of Krypton. "Very clean lines, not cluttered, not cartoony," sums up supervising location manager Bill Doyle.

Absent from the *Daily Planet* building is a golden globe atop its roof. This familiar element would have been a distraction from *Man of Steel*'s "illusion of now" urgency, but that doesn't mean

it's gone entirely. Inside the ground-floor lobby, the globe can be seen as a stylized bronze sculpture.

Interiors for editor-in-chief Perry White's office and the chaotic *Daily Planet* bullpen were shot from the twenty-fifth floor of the Willis Tower, at one point the tallest building in the world. The tower's location on the western edge of Chicago's Loop provided panoramic window views of urban elevation.

To give Metropolis a lived-in feel, the production crew developed enough mementos to overflow a souvenir shop.

ABOVE: General Zod takes in a panoramic view of the Metropolis skyline from the bridge of the Black Zero.

PAGES 158–159: The Black Zero hovers above Metropolis, as, elsewhere in the city, the scout ship arrives shadowing a military aircraft.

These bits of set dressing featured championship banners celebrating the local sports teams, including basketball's Metropolis Generals and the Metropolis Mammoths of pro hockey. Official-looking documents bearing the city's seal reveal the date of its founding in 1661, while police cruisers sport Metropolis's motto: *Veritas et Justitia*. That's Latin for "Truth and Justice," which is a sentiment Superman can readily endorse.

Trouble seems to follow Superman wherever he goes, and it isn't long before Metropolis itself is the latest battleground when a Kryptonian weapon endangers the lives of billions. As the Black Zero takes up position above the heart of downtown Metropolis, directly across the Earth its counterpart deploys in the Indian Ocean.

The two devices become polarized anchors, creating a unique movie effect that is quite different from the standard action-movie climax of progressively bigger explosions. "Right at the source, the effect is really strong," explains Zack Snyder. "It's working at the core of the planet, but at the point of impact it's crushing and flattening everything."

Ultimately, the conflict between Earth and Krypton becomes a showdown between their self-chosen champions. Superman has made his commitment, and an enraged Zod can see no other course than to execute the traitor.

"Zack said, 'I envision this to be a barroom brawl on a larger scale,'" explains Debbie Snyder. "'But I want it to feel just as intimate.' So, as opposed to picking up a beer bottle and whacking the guy over the head, maybe he picks up an I-beam."

The fight between Superman and Zod was logistically complex and relied heavily on digital previsualization— the use of 3-D modeling to render scenes prior to filming. Henry Cavill found the previz process invaluable to him as a performer. "When you're in a green room doing a whole bunch of punches you're thinking, 'Am I on the side of a building? Am I upside down? Am I in space? Am I flying through a building?'" he says. "The previz helps with that."

Fortunately, Zack Snyder's approach to filmmaking was so specific that—even with the seeming spontaneity of the handheld camera—the crew always knew what to expect. "He draws every single specific frame of the movie," says Debbie Snyder. "He has books and books of storyboards. He takes the script and he edits the movie in his head and draws everything as if it was edited: *cut to a close up, cut to a wide shot, cut back to a close up of Clark*. And we use that as the bible. We previz things for visual effects based on Zack's boards, but we sit with our department heads and we go through every shot and every scene."

THESE PAGES: Superman and General Zod trade blows in the streets and skies of Metropolis in an epic battle.

Many of the related action moments in Metropolis required the construction of partial sets in Vancouver. "We shot a tremendous amount of Superman flying through different environments, and we built a tremendous amount of the environments as they were being destructed," says producer Charles Roven. "If the Black Zero was destroying Metropolis, and buildings were crumbling, that was actually shot on a stage. We built all that rubble. We only had to create the environment around it. For the Zod-Superman fight, the foreground of those environments is real; the cars and trucks in those environments are real."

Snyder's team had to juggle the limited time available for shooting with the deadlines required by set construction, and there were many times when the to-do list seemed endless. "One day we literally spread out, on the grass of a cemetery, all the blueprints of all the different sets we had to create in Vancouver, because we had to figure out what the hell we were doing," Roven says. "I think *The Dark Knight Rises* might have been the most logistically complex movie. But this movie—in terms of the production design, prop design, wardrobe design, special effects and floor effects design, and with the wraparound of the visual effects—probably was the most complicated that I've ever worked on. All those elements had to come together like clockwork if it was going to work."

With the partial set construction, other elements in the shot had to be green screened and filled in later with appropriate digital surroundings. By capturing a full 360-degree spherical image of the environment, the VFX crew could later map that image against the appropriate green screen backdrop. "We could save the complicated wirework if we wanted to be in a safe space to do it,"

ABOVE: Superman is tested to his limits by Zod's onslaught.

points out DesJardin. "You can do that back in the stage, back in the warehouse, wherever you have your stunt facility set up. And on the location, you don't need to spend shooting time doing that."

DesJardin's visual effects crew also needed to tackle the more complicated integration of visual effects with moving camera shots, which on *Man of Steel* meant following the bob-and-weave POV of a handheld camera operator. "When you're doing a visual effects shot, you're not setting all that vérité, intimate audience experience aside for the sake of that shot," says co-producer Wes Coller. "You're finding a way of combining them."

The task involved DesJardin lining up his visual effects without the comfort of static, locked-off footage. "Zack chose the cinema vérité thing to make it feel more immediate and more alive," he points out. "My concerns were, if you're handheld photographing a fight between three Kryptonians, there's a chance that you can't

follow a lot of the moves that are about to happen. Because you're a human with a heavy camera, right? And maybe a guy goes a little further on the ground or in the air, and the cameraman has to really adjust or can't quite catch the whole move.

"We can break it down and talk to [camera operator] John Clothier and say, 'Shoot this—but you don't have to follow it.' That's been the biggest challenge: being true to that and yet introducing the Super Hero sci-fi nature of what a fight might be like and your human operator trying to follow this craziness."

Particularly challenging was the moment when Zod and Superman take to the air and their fight continues, unencumbered by gravity or perspective. The crew referred to this sequence as the "hummingbird fight."

"We didn't want to shortchange it," says DesJardin. "Sometimes it's easy to just go, 'Well, this is going to all be CG, because these are really difficult moves. [But] we wanted to anchor it in photography so that when we get to the pauses in the fight, or the moments when your eye is going to dwell on them, it's really them. We wanted the hummingbird fight to be the same, even though they might be at a weird orientation in the space. If somebody wants to come up at a weird angle and punch somebody, they can come up and do it."

DesJardin thinks the one-on-one matchup delivers. "I think as a comics fan, you want to see a flying fistfight," he says. "It's like these two gods basically fighting over the city, causing destruction but mainly taking each other out. That's what you want to get. That's your payoff as a fan."

BELOW: Zod and Superman square off inside the skeleton of a half-completed skyscraper.

RIGHT: The scene depicted in the concept art as it appears in the finished film.

AFTER MULTIPLE GENERATIONS, what do people continue to respond to in the character of Superman? And how did *Man of Steel* reignite that fascination?

It's become cliché to look at Super Hero movies as meditations on power and responsibility, so *Man of Steel* took a different approach. By using General Zod as Superman's antagonist, the film became an examination of nature and nurture, and the value of family.

"There's this tension—will he align himself with these people, or will he align himself with Earth?" asks writer David Goyer. "And really, in a lot of ways, the theme of the film is he's got two fathers.

"To a certain extent, Clark/Kal has grown up with two sets of moral values, two sets of histories. And he needs to choose, to a large extent, whether or not he wants to be a child of Earth or a child of Krypton."

Zack Snyder emphasizes the importance of our planet, specifically the Kansas town of Smallville, in crafting the values of the Last Son of Krypton. "What Martha and Jonathan were able to teach him is something that he has been able to take with him into his adult life," he says, "and that is that his point of view is not *the* point of view. It's *a* point of view. And that's not where Zod is."

Goyer, who worked with Christopher Nolan to develop the stories for *The Dark Knight Trilogy*, points out that *Batman Begins* destroyed one of the main character's talismans by burning Wayne Manor to the ground. Goyer hit a similar beat in *Man of Steel* by devastating Smallville. "[The villains] pick Smallville very specifically because they know it will hit close to home. And they know that on a psychological level it's an attack on [Superman's] innocence. But it's also an attack against the things that make him human. It's very much meant to be an attack against his Earth heritage."

It is Zod who believes that he is the torchbearer of Krypton—the chosen one destined to rekindle the Kryptonian race. And he is convinced that Superman, who has rejected his calling and who possesses the melting-pot genetics of a natural birth, is a threat to everything he holds dear. "It's like a Pocahontas story, and [Superman] joins the savages," says Zack Snyder.

PAGES 168–169: Superman unleashes the full fury of his heat vision.

RIGHT: Shattered glass and pulverized rubble rains down from a skyscraper's upper stories.

PAGES 172–173: Two Kryptonian drop ships make a pass above the Kansas cornfields before zeroing in on the smoking war zone that is Smallville.

Scientists on Earth may have mapped the human genome, but they still haven't determined how much of what makes us unique is genetic and how much is the product of upbringing or willpower. *Man of Steel* presents a blank-slate Superman, someone devoid of the DNA programming that would have assigned him to a caste. And it is exactly that unfinished quality—of not *having* a preordained path—that leaves him vulnerable to Zod's promises of an inescapable future.

"Superman is the ultimate kind of nature-versus-nurture story," says Goyer. "His Kryptonian heritage and his uniquely American heritage. It's not just that Superman grew up on Earth, it's that he grew up with specifically American values. And in the course of the film he's given a choice: Which person does he want to be—the son of Krypton or the son of Earth?"

One possible outcome is presented midway through the film. During a session of nightmarish mental torment, Zod plies his devil's lures on Kal-El and ends his lesson with a vision of Superman sinking beneath a mire of human skulls. Clad in an all-black version of his familiar costume, this dream-state Superman signifies the potential for even the greatest champions to grow corrupt.

THESE PAGES: A frightening depiction of Superman as a tyrant hints at one possible path the character could take.

BELOW: Henry Cavill sinks into a morass of skulls during the shooting of a dream sequence.

"It's not an immediate 'I must stop them,'" says Henry Cavill. "It's quite the opposite. These are my people. This is my one chance to actually belong. What if I do fight them? My gut says I should, and then Earth rejects me. Earth has rejected [Zod] so far, and he hasn't even shown them his full repertoire of strangeness."

Yet Superman is the only Kryptonian conceived by an act of love, and the only parents he has ever known are residents of the American heartland. "He never says *Truth, Justice, and the American Way*," says Zack Snyder, recalling the catchphrase that was introduced to the Superman legend during the radio dramas of the 1940s. "He *could* say it, and it wouldn't be outrageous. In the movie he says, 'I'm American,' and he doesn't apologize for that.

"He knows he cannot be a tool of the American government. But he doesn't deny who he is. He says to the general, 'I grew up in Kansas; I'm as American as you can get.' Which I think is refreshing," Snyder says.

Christopher Nolan, born in London but a naturalized citizen of the U.S., believes that Superman's American upbringing isn't exclusionary, but is in fact one of the factors that makes him so welcoming. "I think Superman stands for the best of America," he says. "He's from another planet, and he's effectively an immigrant. He's part of that story. America is a country that's built on immigration, on the basis of people from all different cultures adding to the notion of what America is."

To deny Superman his American heritage, says Snyder, would be to gut the character's essence. "It's like you've cut his legs off," he says. "Because [then] he has no identity. He lives in no world."

Perhaps the best endorsement of Superman's values comes from the fans who love him, the people who see beyond his status as a movie character or comic book star and perceive the ripples that Superman makes throughout our shared culture. During filming in Plano, Illinois, Henry Cavill frequently made time for local residents who came around to share a handshake. They weren't hoping to meet an actor but instead responded to the cape, the costume, and everything they represented. They wanted to meet the Man of Steel. "They look at me in a certain way, which makes [me] realize the responsibility that is on my shoulders," says Cavill. "And how important it is that I do this right."

Snyder, for one, isn't about to make apologies. "I'm willing to say: This is Superman. Love him or leave him, but this is Superman."

THESE PAGES: It's Superman to the rescue as Henry Cavill strikes a classic Man of Steel pose.

PAGES 178–179: The Black Zero and other vessels of the Kryptonian armada are silhouetted against the enormous setting sun of Rao.

ACKNOWLEDGMENTS

The journey from Kandor to Kansas has been an epic adventure. Zack Snyder and the producers of *Man of Steel* would like to extend a special thank you to all the incredible actors, artists, designers, photographers, technicians, and countless other crew members, who through their wealth of talent and tireless dedication have made it possible to bring this film to life. We are incredibly grateful to have been able to share in the undertaking of this endeavor with each and every one of you. In addition, we would like to express our most sincere gratitude to everyone at Warner Bros., Legendary Pictures, and DC Entertainment who time and time again have shown their enthusiastic support for our films.

CREDITS

COSTUME ILLUSTRATORS
Warren Manser
Keith Christensen
Phillp Boutte Jr.
Ed Natividad
Steve Jung
Constantine Sekeris

ART DEPARTMENT ILLUSTRATORS
Main Unit:
Jaime Jones
Peter Rubin
Richard Buoen
Tani Kunitake
Christian Lorenz Scheurer

Vancouver Unit:
Warren Flanagan
Milena Zdravkovic

WETA WORKSHOP
Creative Director / Co-Owner: Richard Taylor
Workshop Supervisor: Rob Gillies
Head of Production: Grant Bensley
Design Studio Manager: Rik Athorne
Design Studio Coordinator: Chris Lakeman

WETA WORKSHOP DESIGNERS
Andrew Moyes
Adam Anderson
Leri Greer
Aaron Beck
Christian Pearce
Stuart Thomas
Ben Mauro
Long Ouyang
Matthew Rogers

WORKSHOP MODEL MAKERS, MOLDERS, ELECTRONICS, AND PAINTERS
Pietro Marson
Steven Smart
Stephen Edwards
Natalie Munro
Joel Ahie-Drought
Alexander Ingle
Brian Stendebach
Tristan McCallum
Roderick Sheehy
Sourisak Chanpaseuth
Carlos Slater
John Baster

Photography by Clay Enos

WARNER BROS. PICTURES PRESENTS
IN ASSOCIATION WITH LEGENDARY PICTURES A SYNCOPY PRODUCTION A ZACK SNYDER FILM "MAN OF STEEL"
HENRY CAVILL AMY ADAMS MICHAEL SHANNON KEVIN COSTNER DIANE LANE LAURENCE FISHBURNE ANTJE TRAUE AYELET ZURER AND RUSSELL CROWE
MUSIC BY HANS ZIMMER BASED UPON SUPERMAN CHARACTERS CREATED BY JERRY SIEGEL & JOE SHUSTER AND PUBLISHED BY DC ENTERTAINMENT EXECUTIVE PRODUCERS THOMAS TULL LLOYD PHILLIPS JON PETERS
STORY BY DAVID S. GOYER & CHRISTOPHER NOLAN SCREENPLAY BY DAVID S. GOYER PRODUCED BY CHARLES ROVEN CHRISTOPHER NOLAN EMMA THOMAS DEBORAH SNYDER DIRECTED BY ZACK SNYDER

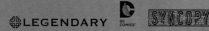

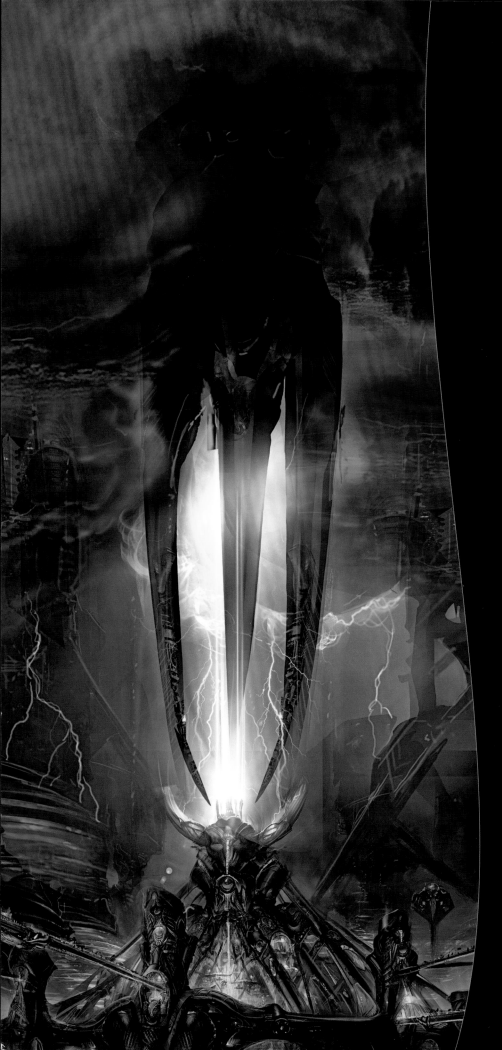

INSIGHT
EDITIONS

PO Box 3088
San Rafael, CA 94912
www.insighteditions.com

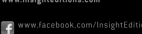 www.facebook.com/InsightEditio

Twitter: @insighteditions

COLOPHON
PUBLISHER: RAOUL GOFF
EDITOR: CHRIS PRINCE
ART DIRECTOR: CHRISSY KWASNI
PRODUCTION MANAGER: ANNA WA

INSIGHT EDITIONS would like to thank Wes C
Adam Forman, Zack Snyder, Deborah Snyder, Ch
Emma Thomas, Christopher Nolan, Josh Anders
Curt Kanemoto, Shane Thompson, Melissa Jolle
Steve Fogelson, Stephanie Mente, Wayne Smith
Elaine Piechowski, Melanie Swartz, Kristen Chi
Jon Glick, and Elaine Ou.

Library of Congress Cataloging-in-Pub
Data available.

ISBN: 978-1-60887-181-0

ROOTS of PEACE   REPLANTED PAPER

Insight Editions, in association with Roots o
plant two trees for each tree used in the ma
this book. Roots of Peace is an internationa
humanitarian organization dedicated to era
mines worldwide and converting war-torn la
productive farms and wildlife habitats. Roo
plant two million fruit and nut trees in Afgha
provide farmers there with the skills and su
sary for sustainable land use.

Manufactured in Hong Kong by Insight Editi

10 9 8 7 6 5 4 3 2 1